Twayne's United States Authors Series

Sylvia E. Bowman, *Editor*

INDIANA UNIVERSITY

Alice Brown

ALICE BROWN

ALICE BROWN

By DOROTHEA WALKER

Nassau Community College,
State University of New York

Twayne Publishers, Inc.   ::   New York

Library of Congress Cataloging in Publication Data

Walker, Dorothea.
    Alice Brown.

        (Twayne United States authors series. TUSAS 239)
        Bibliography: p. 171.
        1.   Brown, Alice, 1857-1948—Criticism and interpretation.
PS1128.W3   818'.5'209   73-17019
ISBN 0-8057-0099-4

To Bill,
whom I love,
and
In Memoriam
Professor Arthur Deering,
who led me to Alice Brown

Preface

The disenchantment of today's youth with traditional values was epitomized for me recently by the remark of one of my students that she didn't want "to read anything that had been written before [she] was born." Yet, today's generation—disillusioned by the result of technological and material progress and by attempts to bring into society such values as affirmation of individual worth, peace among nations, insurance of a habitable environment, love between human beings—is seeking the same ideals that form the fundamental themes of such an "old-fashioned" writer as Alice Brown.

Alice Brown exemplifies these relevant values in her novels, short stories, plays, and poetry—works written throughout more than five decades during which Victorian optimism gave way to twentieth-century pessimism, with two world wars and the Vietnam crisis attesting to the general lack of wisdom in a civilization praising itself for its explosion of knowledge. Because most of her books are out-of-print, Alice Brown remains generally unknown today. To remedy her undeserved obscurity, I have analyzed the best of her work, in order to reveal an artistic vision which, although of another time, continues to concern itself irrevocably with the fundamental needs of humanity. In this first published book-length study of Alice Brown, I have analyzed in detail short stories from her various collections, novels written at different stages in her career, her one Broadway-produced play, and several of her one-act plays. I have analyzed briefly less important works and merely referred to others, when pertinent. All has been done to enhance the reader's understanding of Miss Brown's total contribution to literature and to show her world view as relevant for today.

To the present generation, characterized by its cynicism and its joylessness, as well as by its high ideals, Alice Brown brings a message of hope—not an illusory dream that clouds reality, but a hope, firmly based in psychological truth, that assesses life in its direction and end to find that man indeed makes his own existence. To show that he can make it a satisfying one, Miss Brown spreads before the reader the beauties of the physical world and the realities of the moral one. Her own life, of which I mention merely the facts bearing on her artistic vision, provided not only the substance out of which she wrote but also the example to show the validity of her insight. Critical material on Alice Brown's works has been included only when necessary to give insight into her important works. No attempt has been made to assess her complete work, nor has attention been given to her influence on other writers.

The view of a generation nurtured on pessimism and anxiety should be balanced by a view that insists on optimism and order. As the way in which one views existence determines to a great extent how he will place himself in it, it would be the hope of Alice Brown, as it is my hope, that this book will help to make its reader more at home in his universe.

Many individuals and several libraries have helped to form this book. I wish especially to express my appreciation to Walter Muir Whitehill, director and librarian of the Boston Athenaeum, for his courteous and generous action in making available the long-out-of-print books by Alice Brown; to Elise D. Kruse, reference librarian at the Athenaeum, for her assistance in tracking down difficult information; to John Alden, keeper of rare books at the Boston Public Library, for supplying unpublished letters and the manuscripts of poetic tributes to Miss Brown; to Elizabeth S. Duvall, bibliographer of the Sophia Smith Collection at Smith College Library, for her aid with Miss Brown's letters to Dr. Tallant; to the late Reverend William L. Lucey, S.J., curator of manuscripts, Dinand Library, College of the Holy Cross, Worcester, Massachusetts, for his interest in

Preface

Alice Brown and for his help in providing her extensive correspondence to the Reverend Joseph Mary Lelen; to James M. Mahoney, librarian, Dinand Library, College of the Holy Cross; to Edith Forbes, assistant director of the Nassau Community College Library, and to Mrs. Vera Jerwick, for securing out-of-print books and for rendering comfort as well as assistance; to Edward Darling, editor of the *Unitarian-Universalist World;* to the librarians at Yale University Library; to the editorial department of the *Christian Science Monitor;* to Myron Ritter, secretary, Women's Rest Tour Association; to the Library for the Performing Arts at Lincoln Center; and to Harvard University Library.

My thanks must be expressed to Dr. Susan Toth, who offered interest and encouragement as well as scholarly information, and whose dissertation, *More than Local Color: A Reappraisal of Rose Terry Cooke, Mary Wilkins Freeman and Alice Brown* provided valuable insights into Miss Brown's short stories. My special gratitude must be given to Dr. Paul A. Doyle of Nassau Community College for his unfailing kindness in reading my manuscript as well as for his excellent suggestions. Most of all, I am deeply grateful to Gerry Stauffer, whose friendship sustained me through many weary hours of research, and whose understanding of Alice Brown and the truth of her vision grew with mine.

Dorothea Walker

Nassau Community College
State University of New York
Garden City, Long Island

Acknowledgments

I wish to express my gratitude to the following for permission to quote from unpublished or copyrighted material:

To Thornton Wilder for permission to quote from *The Eighth Day*.

To Boston Public Library for permission to quote from unpublished manuscripts in the collections of the Boston Public Library.

To College of the Holy Cross for permission to quote from the unpublished letters from Alice Brown to Reverend Joseph Mary Lelen and from related letters.

To Harvard University for permission to quote from Miss Brown's letter to Gamaliel Bradford. (Letter quoted by permission of the Harvard College Library.)

To Smith College for permission to quote from the letters in the Sophia Smith Collection, Smith College Library.

To Yale University for permission to quote from the unpublished letters from Alice Brown to Esther Bates and others in the Collection of American Literature, Yale University Library.

To Thomas Y. Crowell Company for permission to quote from *The Reader's Encyclopedia of American Literature* (edited by Max J. Herzberg).

To Doubleday and Company for permission to quote from Peter L. Berger, *A Rumor of Angels*.

To Harper and Row for permission to quote from Pierre Teilhard de Chardin, *Hymn of the Universe*.

To *Life* for permission to quote from "The Youth Commune" by John Stickney, *Life* magazine, July 18, 1969, © 1969, Time, Inc.

To Louisiana State University Press for permission to quote from William Van O'Connor's *Climates of Tragedy*.

To David McKay Company, Inc., for permission to quote from Caroline Bird, *Born Female*. To Laurence Michel and Richard Sewall for permission to quote from *Tragedy: Modern Essays in Criticism*. To the National Council of Teachers of English for permission to quote from George Levine, "Realism, or In Praise of Lying: Some Nineteenth-Century Novels," *College English* (January, 1970). To W. W. Norton & Co., Inc. for permission to quote from Karen Horney, *Feminine Psychology*. To Lyle Stuart, Inc., for permission to quote from Albert Ellis, *Reason and Emotion in Psychotherapy*. To *The New York Times* for permission to quote from Edward B. Fiske "Religion" (January 4, 1970) © 1970 by The New York Times Company. Reprinted by permission. To Van Nostrand Reinhold Company for permission to quote from Alexander Cowie, *The Rise of the American Novel*, © 1951 by Litton Educational Publishing, Inc., by permission of Van Nostrand Reinhold Company, and from *American Local Color Stories* by Harry R. Warfel and G. Harrison Orians, © 1941, by Litton Educational Publishing, Inc., by permission of Van Nostrand Reinhold Company. To the World Publishing Company for permission to quote from Gordon Rattray Taylor, *The Biological Time Bomb*,© World Publishing Company.

Contents

Chronology

1857   Alice Brown born in Hampton Falls, New Hampshire, December 5; daughter of (Elizabeth and Lucas) Levi Brown.

1876   Graduated from Robinson Academy, Exeter, New Hampshire.

1876-
1880   Taught school in a country academy.

1880   Accepted position on staff of *Christian Register* in Boston.

1885   Joined staff of *The Youth's Companion* in Boston.

1890   Toured England for five months with Louise Imogen Guiney.

1891   Founded "Women's Rest Tour Association." Mrs. Julia Howe was first president.

1892   Founded magazine *Pilgrim Script.*

1894   *Three Heroines of New England Romance* (with Louise Imogen Guiney and Harriet Prescott Spofford).

1895   Took a ten-week walking tour with Louise Imogen Guiney in Wales, Shropshire, and Devon. *Meadow-Grass: Tales of New England Life.*

1896   *Robert Louis Stevenson* (A study written with Louise Imogen Guiney). *By Oak and Thorn* (description of tour of England). *Women of Colonial and Revolutionary Times—Mercy Warren. The Road to Castaly* (collection of poetry).

1897   *The Day of His Youth.*

1899   *Tiverton Tales.*

1900-
1920   Published more than 130 short stories in magazines such as *The Atlantic Monthly, Harper's, Harper's Bazaar, Scribner's, McClure's, Lippincott's, Outlook*

Woman's Home Companion, Delineator, Collier's, as well as scattered essays and poems.

1901 *Kings End. Margaret Warrener.*

1904 *High Noon. Judgment.*

1905 *Paradise.*

1906 *The County Road.*

1908 Contributed Chapter XI to *The Whole Family* (novel by twelve authors). *Rose MacLeod.*

1909 *The Story of Thyrza.*

1910 *Country Neighbors. John Winterbourne's Family.*

1911- President of "Women's Rest Tour Association."
1948

1912 *My Love and I. The Secret of the Clan, a Story for Girls.*

1913 *Vanishing Points* (collection of short stories). *Robin Hood's Barn.* Joined Boston Authors' Club.

1914 Won Winthrop Ames prize of $10,000 for *Children of Earth: A Play of New England. Mella's Tramp* (one-act play) produced in Pennsylvania with Cornelia Otis Skinner.

1915 *Children of Earth: A Play of New England* produced on Broadway (opened January 12 with Miss Effie Shannon in leading role).

1916 *The Prisoner.*

1917 *Bromley Neighborhood.*

1918 *The Flying Teuton and Other Stories.*

1919 *The Black Drop.*

1920 *Homespun and Gold* (collection of short stories). *The Wind Between the Worlds.*

1920- President of Boston Authors' Club.
1923

1921 *One-Act Plays. Louise Imogen Guiney.*

1922 *Old Crow.*

1923 *Ellen Prior.*

1924 *Charles Lamb: A Play.*

1925 *The Mysteries of Ann.*

1927 *Dear Old Templeton.*

1929 *The Golden Ball* (a play).

1930 Friendship with the Reverend Joseph Mary Lelen, Glenmary Missioners, Glendale, Ohio.

Chronology

1931 The short story "A March Wind" dramatized for radio.
      The Marriage Feast (a play).
1932 *Kingdom in the Sky.*
1934 *Jeremy Hamlin.*
1935 *The Willoughbys.*
1939 *Fable and Song.*
1944 *Pilgrim's Progress.*
1948 Died June 21, in Boston.

Alice Brown

CHAPTER *1*

In The New England Tradition

"N EW England sunshine on your loom" is part of Mary
Godwin's poetic tribute in honor of Alice Brown's
sixty-fourth birthday,[1] and it indicates that friends and
fellow writers considered Alice Brown and New England to
be inseparable. It is not surprising, then, that in any
consideration of the literary contribution of Miss Brown,
prominent mention is made of her New England background, which is undoubtedly the reason she is grouped
with such New England writers as Sarah Orne Jewett, Rose
Terry Cooke, and Mary E. Wilkins Freeman—all her con-
temporaries, although Rose Terry Cooke died when Alice
Brown was thirty-five years old and barely beginning her
long, prosperous literary career. Specifically, Alice Brown
is said to have "followed in Sarah Orne Jewett's literary
footsteps,"[2] which of course may be true, although such
grouping, instead of enhancing an original talent, deni-
grates it, particularly when the group consists of "wom-
en writers." Alice Brown's talent surpasses that of those
in the grouping, for her inventiveness in character and plot
and her insight into motives and desires led her not only
to psychologically valid conclusions but also to a presentation of these conclusions in artistically pleasing images.

I *Early Life and Influences*

Though it is not fair to dismiss Alice Brown as a local-
color regionalist writer, it must be understood that her life
cannot be separated from her work; for her New England
background formed the first images of characters and events,

scenes and atmosphere, she was to use in depicting characters like Mrs. Blair and Miss Dyer in "Joint Owners in Spain," or Farmer Eli in "Farmer Eli's Vacation." Since she had known these characters "in the flesh . . . to paint the picture at all she must paint it as it was in her heart. To add to it or to subtract from it were to violate truth itself."[3] And this background centered around Hampton Falls, New Hampshire, a typical New England farming community six miles from the sea, where her parents, Levi and Elizabeth (Lucas) Brown, owned the small farm on which Alice Brown was born December 5, 1857. Her father was the grandson of Abraham Brown and Judith Runnels, an Indian, whom Levi strongly resembled. His brother Sewell, a cobbler and shoemaker, went to Portsmouth in 1814; but another brother, Fred, apparently farmed the land, as did Alice Brown's father.

The ancestors of Alice Brown were of early New England stock. *The History of Hampton Falls* notes that a Noah Brown (who never married), son of the Indian Judith Runnels, was vicious "having the bad qualities of both races; he was supported by the town during his last days."[4] As Miss Brown remained remarkably uncommunicative in regard to herself through many years of successful authorship,[5] very little more can be stated definitely about her forebears.[6] It seems safe to assume, however, that the pioneer spirit ran deep in her veins.

Nostalgically recalling an idyllic early life, Alice Brown gives a glimpse of the little schoolhouse she attended—"not 'red' as tradition likes it"—where she memorized sums in the old-fashioned way and also spoke pieces at the "prim, tremulous ordeal of 'last day,' when all the parents come and a committee man makes a gruff speech." But sums and parsing were enlivened by "making playhouses by the roadside, with sticks and stones."[7] The playhouse, which lingered long in her memory, became a place for lovers' meetings in her stories and novels. And the little "not red" schoolhouse is undoubtedly commemorated in "Number Five," the opening essay in *Meadow-Grass: Tales of New England Life.*[8]

Upon graduation from the schoolhouse, young Alice enrolled at Robinson Seminary in Exeter.[9] This "ladies' seminary" was situated four miles from her home, and she walked twice each day, except when winter weather prohibited. She loved the lonely road in spite of dire predictions of a "predestinating, prophetic old lady" who always hoped for the worst and who convinced her that the lonely walk was sure to result in "slaughter too gruesome to be more than ominously implied in head shakes and muttered implications." By that time "embarked in the littlest of crafts on the ecstasies of poetry," she repeated to herself some lines about "One that on a lonesome road/Doth walk in fear and dread."[10]

Apart from the lessons learned at Robinson Academy, Alice increased her storehouse of knowledge from life itself for the later portrayal of scenes and characters in her novels and tales, her short stories and plays. As Blanche Colton Williams points out, one can deduce from the Tiverton stories that young Alice saw, remembered, and used such customs of her childhood as the looming of rugs and covers; the baking of biscuits, pies, doughnuts; the storing of pork and apples; the keeping of butter. The native flowers, the clove pink, the larkspur,[11] and the ladies' delight, must have been a source of great joy to her; for they appear over and over in her stories. More important, she observed the people, for the clarity with which she describes them can only have come from sharp perception and vivid memory. The village witch of her creation undoubtedly speaks Alice Brown's philosophy when she indicates that staying home doing housewifely tasks limits the vision to home and blinds one to the knowledge of the world outside.[12]

That the outdoors Alice Brown breathed in her young adulthood became of vast importance in her later writings can clearly be seen, for the outdoors constantly sets her tales; the young characters in *Bromley Neighborhood* live, love, laugh, and solve their problems in the midst of the beauties of the natural countryside as the changing scenes of nature mirror the bloom and the decay of lives. And more important, the outdoors becomes a healing power, a value Alice Brown absorbed perhaps as much through her own experience as through her studies of William Wordsworth

and John Keats and other Romantic poets she admired; for
John Winterbourne of *John Winterbourne's Family* leads
his wife, suffering from a nervous breakdown, to the Valley
of the Birds to "lie in the lap of the woods and be mothered
by the great kindness of the air."[13] *In Rose MacLeod,*
Osmond, who is physically deformed but spiritually upright,
has been saved by his grandmother who gave him the earth
to till and who "drained herself for him . . . tended him
and lived the hardiest life with him because he needed it
. . . six months of several years . . . she took him to the
deep woods, and they camped, and she did tasks his heart
bled to think of, as he grew up, and looked at her work-worn
hands; but those things which bound them indissolubly were
never spoken of between them."[14]

And Osmond, when a man, still lives in a shack in the
woods where he finds his strength and health in planting
and harvesting; for to Alice Brown, nature is solace, beauty,
and healing—a force that counteracts the pain, the ugliness,
the destruction caused by the evil of men. Like Henry David
Thoreau, whose *Walden* takes its breath from the close relationship between man and nature, Alice Brown never lost
sight of man's dependence on his natural environment.
Undoubtedly she found in *Walden,* if not her actual inspiration, a way of looking at man and nature with which she
could not only sympathize but understand as a common
New England heritage.[15]

Although Keats, John Milton, Dante Gabriel Rossetti, and
Alfred Lord Tennyson brought her great delight, Wordsworth became her model; for his vision of nature was akin
to her own experience. Subconsciously, she absorbed the
rhythms of poetry as she began to feel its beauty and power,
leading her friends later to expect much from her poetic
power.[16] At the academy, she also studied some Latin but no
Greek, a lack she laments: "I myself regret very much having
had so little Latin—and that taught in a dry way—and I shall
always long for Greek."[17]

Graduating from Robinson Academy in 1876, Alice Brown
began to teach. She explains her difficulties in an autobiographical sketch: ". . . and you teach in a country academy
and are humiliated before the big boys who want to be taught

bookkeeping . . . and you don't know how and haven't yet learned to live unabashed with your ignorances and brazen them out. . . . So . . . you pick up your petticoats . . . you scud off to Boston and into the very odd precincts of the mind where books are written. . . . And since people seem to have a liking for New England stories, you fall into the habit of writing them, perhaps because they are so easy to do. . . . you don't have to try very hard to remember what country-bred men and women are likely to feel."[18]

Nevertheless, courage was required to give up the certainties of teaching for the uncertainties of writing. And perhaps even more courage was required to sever home and family bonds for independence when doing so was the last thing expected of, or desired in, a woman.[19] The provincialism of small-town life did not lend itself to the imagination that later attempted an explanation of existence itself; and although Miss Brown's stories of rural life contain warmth and humor, a hint of the narrowness of the lives described in them underlies the positive values. But Boston, the mecca of writers, lured; and Alice Brown left the farm to make her fortune.

II *Boston and Fame*

Like the struggling young writers Alice Brown portrays in *Margaret Warrener,* she accepted hackwork on a magazine both for experience and for money. She accepted a position on the staff of the *Christian Register,*[20] where she remained until 1885, when she joined the staff of *The Youth's Companion*[21] and "had charge of the department edited with scissors and paste brush."[22] Speaking about this early experience in an interview in 1915, she says, "I've been battered good and hard. . . . I have had my share of bad luck. But nobody amounts to anything if the sailing is always easy. . . . When life is too soft for us, we don't ever amount to much." She also relates that for years she "edited and rewrote 'interesting facts' for *The Youth's Companion,* taking incidents and various curious things from papers all over the country and writing paragraphs over them," and also doing "little stories and verse for the *Christian Register.*"[23] This magazine experience "broadened rather than deepened her; it gave her that catholicity and multiplicity of mind that has made her published list such a miscellany of excellence."[24] The deepening process began in the following decade of her life, for in addition to editing, she wrote and she traveled. The dramatic element grew as the tragic entered her work. She rewrote several of her short stories later as plays, thus attesting to their dramatic competency.[25]

Louise Imogen Guiney, who had long held a belief in her friend's talent, wrote in 1887 that Alice wrote three times as much as she printed, that she was completely an artist and lover of literature, and that she had no concern at all for the earning of her daily bread.[26] Although ample evidence exists that Alice Brown's writing brought her more than her daily bread—in fact, afforded her an excellent living—Miss Brown would agree with Miss Guiney's assessment of lofty attitude, as many of her novels attest. Martin Redfield (*My Love and I*) prostitutes his art in a conflict between idealism and materialism, and Osmond (*Rose MacLeod*) insists that his artist brother Peter use his genius to create, and thereby leave mundane necessities to the ungifted, such as Osmond, who would till the soil devotedly to finance the artistic career of his brother.

The close friendship existing between Miss Guiney and Miss Brown led to their journeying to England together in 1890 to spend five months exploring the English countryside. Alice Brown's *By Oak and Thorn*, published in 1896, contains detailed descriptions of this trip with many nostalgic accounts of the search for literary landmarks of beloved writers, as the Land of the Doones, the Land of Arthur, and Bronte Country. An interesting critical comment appears in *By Oak and Thorn:* "Fiction is not portraiture, but it may easily become a record of those fleeting impressions which make an intrinsic part of the mental tissue. Names familiar to the writer's youth have a way of creeping into her works —nooks and corners, remarkable for no story of their own, crop up when her dreams demand actual habitat."[27] The "fleeting impressions" referred to, particularly of Miss Brown's childhood, "crop up" later to lend authenticity to her New England tales.

A sequel to the 1890 trip came five years later when Miss

Brown and Miss Guiney walked for ten weeks in Wales, Shropshire, and Devon. Their enthusiasm for traveling abroad resulted in the founding of the "Women's Rest Tour Association" and its magazine *Pilgrim Scrip*,[28] whose purpose was to encourage other women to take such a vacation in a foreign land, with pack and stick.[29] Although Miss Brown recognized that women might be in need of a "rest tour," she obviously did not concern herself with the feminist movement of her time. The happiest women in her stories accept a life of service to their families and tacitly acknowledge the husband as head of the household—an idea that appears in a letter written to Dr. Alice Tallant, a young friend with whom she corresponded from the time of Alice Tallant's entrance into college (Smith, 1897).

In speaking of Lucy Stone's daughter, whom they named (for some reason Alice Brown couldn't remember—the letter is written at age ninety) Isaac and who now can't see to write, Alice Brown says: "You're not old enough to have had a glimpse of her mother—Lucy Stone, was she, the A-one Woman's Righter and the roundest, pinkest, pollenest Femina as ever was. I should think her mere charms would have been an argument against her—showing the world that she's not really anything to ask of it when pink cheeks were, from all points of view, enough."[30] Lucy Stone (1818-93), the American reformer and eloquent anti-Slavery lecturer, led the fight for woman suffrage. When she married H. B. Blackwell in 1855, she kept her maiden name, thus giving rise to the expression "Lucy Stone Leaguers"—women who kept their maiden names when they married.

Certainly far from a militant feminist, Alice Brown appears to have been satisfied with woman's place in man's society; for although she explores time and time again the relationship between the sexes, she does so with no apparent protest about man, the strong head, and woman, the loving heart of the relationship. She did find the straight-laced New England attitude toward women humorous and stifling, for she writes again from a summer vacation spot that it is raining hard and the house is full of "dear pottering old maiden ladies"; and she wonders what they would say if she went out in the rain. Finding them "delicious," she reveals that

one put up her hand to her mouth and "whispered mysteriously—there being a *MAN* on the piazza—that she had
been obliged to take off her *flannel petticoat*"—and she
whispered the last two words as if "they were at least evidence of a murder." Again, an old lady confided to her that
the little piles of cow manure were "dreadful—it would be
so embarrassing to walk there with a gentleman!" Miss
Brown concludes that the "free and easy manners of camp
would lift her dear gray hair off her poll."[31]

But Alice Brown's buoyant sense of enjoyment in life
appears to have been sufficient to hold her pen to the genial-
ity of a Charles Dickens rather than to force it to the bitter-
ness of a Jonathan Swift; her weapon attacked with gentle
mockery, and then only seldom. For the most part, life was
too real, too earnest, too beautiful for complaints. Yet the
conventional restrictions of Victorian society did not fail to
influence her writing. Nowhere do harsh or vulgar images
appear, and sexual relationships are explored only from a
spiritual point of view.

However, man's laws and conventions as they conflict
with God's laws and as they specifically pertain to women
do come under her scrutiny; for she contributed to a curious
little volume, *Three Heroines of New England Romance*
(1894), in which she, Harriet Prescott Spofford, and Louise
Imogen Guiney presented the "true stories" of Priscilla
Alden, Agnes Surriage, and Martha Hilton, "with many
little picturings authentic and fanciful by Edmund H.
Garrett."[32] In presenting the facts in the life of Agnes Surriage, the accepting, docile, common-law wife of Sir Harry
Frankland, who endures willingly the pain of ostracism,
Miss Brown hints at the conflict between man's natural
desires and society's laws, a conflict she later explores in
many of her novels—notably in *Paradise,* in which Malory
marries Lindy for the sole purpose of giving her baby a
name, even though he has not fathered the child; and in
The Story of Thyrza, in which the unmarried Thyrza refuses to give her child for adoption. There is no doubt that
Alice Brown stands on the side of the soiled angels.

Thoroughly imbued with New England images and tradition and gently mellowed with Old World charm and values,

Alice Brown gained her first recognition through stories that combine traditional New England values with a rejection of New England Puritanism. *Meadow-Grass* (1895), her first volume of short stories, contains tales presumably of the Hampton Falls neighborhood of her childhood. Fred Lewis Pattee gives two reasons for the acclaim won by them: (1) Miss Brown *knows* the characters she creates, and (2) New England dialect tales enjoyed extreme popularity at the time.[33] Even though there might be some controversy concerning the lasting literary value of these New England tales, there is no doubt that they enjoyed extreme popularity. *Tiverton Tales* (1889) and other important collections, such as *The County Road* and *Country Neighbors*, appeared soon after the first volume. Between 1990 and 1920, more than one hundred and thirty of her stories appeared in popular periodicals.[34]

Apparently writing without surcease at this time, Alice Brown produced an astonishing and varied list. She wrote a study of Robert Louis Stevenson with Louise Imogen Guiney (1895); *The Road to Castaly*, a volume of poetry (1895); the life of Mercy Otis Warren (1896); and numerous novels. She also contributed Chapter XI to *The Whole Family* (1908), a novel by twelve authors, others of whom include William Dean Howells, Mary E. Wilkins Freeman, and Henry James.[35] Although Alice Brown considered herself primarily as a poet, the bulk of her achievement rests in the novels; the most enduring, the short stories; the most famous, the drama. An assessment of Alice Brown, the weaver of New England atmosphere and culture, starts naturally with her short stories.

CHAPTER 2

Local-Color and Beyond

"THERE, in plain people and in common clay, / You find the treasure which the chosen see" is the poetic tribute of Susanne Alice Roulett to the madrigal of birthday verses in honor of Alice Brown, and it emphasizes that not until 1967, when Professor Clarence Gohdes selected *Tiverton Tales* (1899), *The County Road* (1906), and *Meadow-Grass* (1895) to be reprinted for the Americans in Fiction series, did anyone see fit to bring into the current scene this long-buried part of the American heritage in fiction. Professor Gohdes' choice of Alice Brown's stories was influenced by her faithful depiction of the New England scene, and it is for this that mention is given her by literary historians and students of the short story.

The "treasure" first appeared with *Meadow-Grass* (1895) and *Tiverton Tales* (1899)—stories published at the same time as those from Mary E. Wilkins Freeman and Sarah Orne Jewett. Although Miss Brown is usually grouped with both of these authors and although she felt herself to be Miss Jewett's "great lover, far off,"[1] at least one critic felt in 1910 that she surpassed Miss Jewett in that "Sarah Orne Jewett had exquisite craftsmanship and lacked the force of genius; Alice Brown has genius and the craftsman's skill combined."[2] In 1922, Grant Overton pronounced her "without any question [to be] one of the half dozen best short story writers America possesses at this time."[3] Most of the stories later published in collections had first appeared in the best popular magazines of the era,[4] but in the following decades the stories disappeared from critical view, and only a few, notably "Farmer Eli's Vacation" and "A Day Off," have

[30]

lived on in anthology. The reprinting of *Tiverton Tales, The County Road,* and *Meadow-Grass* enables the present generation to become acquainted with Miss Brown's New England tales. All who read them enjoy them; and for Alice Brown this reaction would have been sufficient. Before analyzing the reason for this enjoyment, a brief exploration must be made of the genre called "local-color stories"; for Alice Brown's use of its characteristics led to the selection of *Tiverton Tales, The County Road,* and *Meadow-Grass* for republication.

The period of the local-color writers ranged approximately from the 1870's through the 1890's. Among the earliest were Thomas Bailey Aldrich, Constance Fenimore Woolson, and Bret Harte. Some others consciously employing this technique include George Washington Cable, Charles Egbert Craddock, Mary E. Wilkins Freeman, Thomas Nelson Page, Sarah Orne Jewett, Margaret Deland, Kate Chopin, Harriet Beecher Stowe, Rose Terry Cooke; and these authors represent various sections of America. The most famous of the New England local colorists are Freeman, Jewett, Cooke, and Brown. Most of the writers preferred the short story rather than the novel as a medium, but many of the same characters appear in both short story and novel, as they do in the work of Alice Brown.

Local-color stories portray seriousness of form in sombre colors; decline and decay mirror the passing away of a generation. Set ordinarily in remote villages, the stories present individuals trapped by their failure to find opportunities for individual economic improvement or relief from crushing personal problems, so that they bear harsh burdens for long years. Many of the characters are old; many are lovers unable to marry; but all of them are strongly individualized. A quiet stoicism comes from lives lived close to God and to nature as they reveal a strong sense of personal integrity, loyalty, and adherence to duty.[5]

The writers of this genre ordinarily depict beautiful scenery and reveal their own nostalgia for these departing times. They surround their tales with "atmosphere," with poetic descriptions, with the customs of the locale, and with speech peculiarities of the local inhabitants whose stories they tell.

The result of the selection of characters, customs, and style tends to stories which are retrospective rather than vitally of the moment.[6]

Yet, local color may be considered "one type of realism, if realism be defined as a graphic delineation of actual life. It is concerned with contemporary social truth. Yet it is not a realism that professes to present the whole truth and then proceeds to reveal only the nether side of life without its compensations: its sense of humor, its homiletic tendencies, its forthrightness, and its essential neighborliness. These, too, are the truth, if only partially so, and upon these truths the local colorist seized, sometimes with sentiment, sometimes with austerity."[7]

The type of Realism exemplified in the local-color stories gave way early in the twentieth century, and certainly by 1920, to fiction concerned with social motives and the intense Realism of such writers as Willa Cather, Sherwood Anderson, and Sinclair Lewis;[8] but even though Alice Brown wrote into this period and beyond, she disliked this "intense Realism," particularly as written by such writers as Sinclair Lewis, and remained true to what she considered a finer artistry. The tendency seen at the end of the nineteenth century for the author to "abdicate his office as judge of humanity and to become instead a mere observer or recorder of the somewhat lugubrious human comedy being acted before him"[9] does not appear in the stories of Alice Brown. Instead, the type of Realism inherent in the local-color technique served her well; and if merit "depends upon an author's knowledge, insight, and artistry,"[10] Miss Brown merits praise because her atmosphere and her point of view are her own. Her best stories deserve revival not only for their literary interest in a time long since passed, but rather because they contain "vivid, lively accounts of human dilemmas."[11]

In Alice Brown's accounts of these human dilemmas, she never lost her Victorian virtue of hope; even though a modern reader might feel momentary irritation about the acceptance a character shows for going on alone in the same familiar way, such as Amelia in "A Second Marriage" who, in a story reminiscent of Mary E. Wilkins Freeman's "A

New England Nun," decides to forego life with a former sweetheart in order to keep alive the way of life she had learned during fifteen years of marriage to an elderly husband. But the choice is freely made; Amelia will be happy, implies Alice Brown. The decision is made in the context of full knowledge of the transitoriness of life and not in an illusory context that there is no death.

Alice Brown may be placed in the group of local-color writers because of her remote village settings, her depiction of the elderly; particularly elderly lovers long kept apart; her use of nature as a vital force; and her stress on the individual who shows personal integrity, loyalty, and adherence to duty. Like Sarah Orne Jewett's stories, Alice Brown's reveal a deep appreciation of nature and of country life; like Rose Terry Cooke's, her tales are filled with idiosyncratic characters; like Mary E. Wilkins Freeman's, her themes are often of individual rebellion.[12] But above and beyond these likenesses, Alice Brown's New England tales are marked with a humor and a psychological acuteness that are purely her own.

In a letter written in 1921 to Gamaliel Bradford, Alice Brown indicates that she loves the Greek spirit and many other things outside New England; but she confesses that "New England was my primer, my 'copy' first set me, and perhaps I can get nearer the reality which ought to be letters by sticking to it. . . ."[13] Not surprisingly, then, her finest achievement in the short story genre remains the New England tales, even though her moralistic love stories and parables represent a poetic searching for form. And the local-color tenets, far from restricting her art, free her to transcend narrow limits to pose truth pertinent to men and women of all time. The stories chosen for analysis from her best collections—*Meadow-Grass, Tiverton Tales, The County Road,* and *Country Neighbors*—present this truth.

I *New England Tales*

Alice Brown, although admitting that she wrote New England stories because they were easy to do and because people liked them, also recognized that regional stories tend to serve a sociological purpose: "Every bit of fiction setting forth the 'form and pressure' of unspoiled country life with fidelity and insight, becomes a valuable contribution not only to art, but to social science. To keep alive tradition and the habits of speech of an older generation is to enrich the folk-lore of fiction; and it is greatly to be desired that England and America should multiply these homely records of a time now becoming fugitive before a strenuous and complex civilization."[14]

Exactly how "strenuous and complex" the civilization would become seven decades later (with man's steps on the moon) had not even been dreamed of when these words were written. However, the sociological and historical significance of these regional tales, important though it is, pales beside their ability to comment significantly about the human condition. Relevance is found in the psychological truths that form the basis of these stories as well as the foundation of modern living. Transcending New England, America, and the Western World, these stories shed some light on man's actions as man.

In a discussion of *Meadow-Grass,* Horace Scudder notes that it has "remained for Miss Brown to enter this same general field of New England country life, and without producing any new variety of tale, or scarcely any new character, to use familiar material, and yet illumine it with a new light. We cannot define it any more than by saying that the genuine humor which pervades the best of her work is closely identified with a love of sunshine, of growing things, and of movement in nature and the corresponding changes of light and shade in the human soul."[15] Curiously, half a century or more later, the late Herman J. Muller of Indiana University, one of the earliest workers in the field of genetics, comprised a list of desirable qualities which might be bred into man in the future and included "appreciation of nature."[16] Other qualities listed as desirable by Muller are "moral courage and cooperative disposition . . . and aptness of expression." In referring to these qualities, Gordon Rattray Taylor comments that "there is much evidence that these are the product at least as much of environment as of heredity."[17]

When these qualities are chosen by scientists, not humanists or artists, the relevance of Miss Brown's moral vision becomes self-evident; for the principal characters in the short stories collected in *Meadow-Grass* display an "appreciation of nature" so ingrained that it molds and matures them quite as much as their own considered actions; they show "moral courage" so strong that it overcomes natural timidity and shyness; they reveal "cooperative disposition" so fine that catastrophes in human relationships become nonexistent; they speak with "aptness of expression" so genuine that what they say very often reveals the deep-seated motivation far more clearly than what they do. Indeed, Herman Muller's choice of the highest attributes of human nature mirrors Alice Brown's.

As is natural in the local-color genre, the stories build themselves on incident rather than a complicated plot; and the selected incident turns the tale by revealing a facet of human behavior, by resolving the life, or the problem in the life, in the light of eternal truth as Miss Brown sees it. A good example in *Meadow-Grass* is the much-anthologized "Farmer Eli's Vacation." After dreaming about a trip to see the ocean for many years, Farmer Eli, together with his wife, his daughter, and his son-in-law, prepares to make the journey, a fairly easy one of several hours' driving. Although Eli has lived with the dream which "in his starved imagination was like a dream of the Acropolis to an artist stricken blind, or as mountain outlines to the dweller in a lonely plain" and has been full of plans and happiness for days before the great event, now on the eve of departure, "he shrank back from it, with an undefined notion that it was like death, and that he was not prepared."[18]

However, the family leaves early next morning—Eli, rather timidly; his wife, bustling and important—and is determined to enjoy the long-awaited trip. As they enjoy a picnic lunch on the way, they note in some satisfaction that the land leading to the ocean compares less and less favorably with their own. At last they reach the dunes, beyond which lies the ocean. His daughter, Hattie, sensitive in the same way as her father, takes his arm and leads him over the dunes for a glimpse of the sea, which, when he turns to look at it, he faced "as a soul might face Almighty Greatness,

only to be stricken blind thereafter; for his eyes filled pain-
fully with slow, hot tears."[19] Eli and his daughter look at
the sea, chilled but content, until suppertime; and when his
wife asks him whether the sea fulfills his expectations, Eli
replies gently that he guesses it does.

That night he lies facing the sea, although he cannot see
it; waiting for dawn, he does not sleep all night. At the first
rays of light, he gets up and tells his daughter, who had got
up to see the sunrise, that "I jest come out to see how 'twas
here, before I go. I'm goin' home, I'm goin' *now*."[20] And
before his wife even gets up, Eli starts alone for home; arriv-
ing back at his farm in early evening, he answers the as-
tonishment of his hired man's question, "What's busted?"
with "Oh, nothin'," leaping from the wagon as if twenty
years had been taken from his bones. "I guess I'm too old
for such jaunts. I hope you didn't forgit them cats."[21]

Although some critics point to the obvious moral in many
of Alice Brown's stories, "Farmer Eli's Vacation" stands as
a delicately etched tale, shadowy, ambiguous. Nowhere
does the author even hint at a reason for Eli's strange behavior. The reader must conjecture, according to his own
experience, whether the reality of his dream proved greater
than Eli could bear, whether the habit of home could not
sustain a wider vision, or whether the conflict between both
refused reconciliation. Certainly the paradoxical nature
of an achieved aspiration underlies this story; but the meaning shimmers, constantly eluding the reader's intellectual
grasp. Farmer Eli, gentle and diffident, a man who has
achieved a lifelong dream, stands, however, as a monument
to the artistry of Alice Brown.

Contrary to Eli, who achieves his individuality by tapping
its inner šources while remaining outwardly the conventional farmer, Delilah Joyce of "At Sudleigh Fair" achieves
hers by throwing over conventional conformity. Not caring
about the norms of housewifery, she has no care for which
day she washes, nor for normal order, although she is
"fastidiously neat." But her rebellion takes such an
innocent form as defying the classified system of hanging
clothes on the line. She declares that "a petticoat'll dry jest
as quick if it's hung 'side of a nightgown. . . . An' when

you come to hangin' stockin's by the pair, better separate 'em, I say! Like man an' wife! Give 'em a vacation, once in a while, an' love'll live the longer!"[22]

Because of Dilly's procrastinating habits and her eccentric behavior, such as taking her meals under a tree and roaming the countryside at odd hours, she earns a reputation as a witch, albeit a good one. Her foresightedness stems from the perception that freedom from hampering habit has given her and from the knowledge that wandering through woods and fields has supplied. She not only knows everything that goes on, but adequately supplies cause and effect when necessary, as when she tells young Molly, "there's a good deal missed when ye stay to home makin' pies, an' a good deal ye can learn if ye live out-door."[23]

And what Dilly learns, she puts to good use, always with the end to straightening out problems and helping to put order into disorderly lives. When she advises Farmer Tolman to give his son Davie more time to go fishing and to drive the cows to pasture himself if he wants to prevent their drying up, the prescription works, not because Dilly has occult powers, but because she has seen young Davie running the cows back and forth to pasture so that he could find stolen time for fishing. The seemingly magical powers are also put to work to solve her young friend Molly's problem; for Elvin Drew, Molly's love, has changed into a morose, taciturn, troubled young man. Dilly hints mysteriously to Elvin that his trouble will not pass until he has confessed his actions; otherwise, he will be "a stranger among your own folks, an' a wanderer on the earth till you tell."[24] But common sense and observation rather than witchcraft have provided the insight into Elvin's problem; for on one of her nocturnal meanderings, Dilly has seen Elvin setting fire to his house, presumably to collect the insurance. Like an avenging angel (although a kind and humorous one), Dilly succeeds in getting Elvin to confess his transgression and take his punishment, so that he can tell his sweetheart Molly that "things of this world ain't everything. Even freedom ain't everything. There's something better."[25]

And Dilly also helps ease Molly's heartbreak over the coming forced separation by assuring her that Molly can help her lover by keeping him in her mind all day long, for then her "sperit'll go right through the stone walls, if they put him there, an' cheer him up," because even though people don't know "why they're uplifted sometimes, when there ain't no cause; but . . . it's other folk's love."[26] The unconventional, the procrastinating witch Dilly succeeds in wisdom; for she lives close to its source, as she invites Molly to come to her and "eat up the woods an' drink up the sky."[27] In complete renunciation of conventional Puritan ideas about wrongdoing, Dilly assures Elvin that "there ain't nothin' to be afraid of but wrong-doin', an' that's only a kind of sickness we al'ays git well of. An' God A'mighty's watchin' over us all the time. An' if you've sp'iled your chance in this life, don't you mind. There's time enough. Plenty o' time, you says to yourself, plenty!"[28]

In addition to emphasizing the wisdom which outdoor living and neighborly caring brings to good witches such as Dilly, Alice Brown also draws attention to the transience of life in an orderly universe in which the love of God for man, as well as the love of man for God, will help to give courage to endure hardship as well as wisdom to overcome it. Unlike the importance-of-the-moment philosophy, the vision of these New England characters encompasses birth, life, and death; but more important, it includes the knowledge that neighbor must help neighbor, friend must help friend. Psychiatrist Joost A. M. Meerloo believes that the "man who reveals his despair wants, first of all, human contact, empathy and sympathy. He wants a certain form of spontaneous self-analysis that comes about by having a listening ear. Every friend can temporarily provide that."[29] Alice Brown also believes that ordinary people can serve as curers of psychological and emotional ills; but these people must be, like Dilly, wise and loving.

In contrast to Dilly, who joyfully serves her fellow man by removing his psychological problem, Amanda in "A Righteous Bargain" serves her family by easing its physical problems but repressing her own desire for fulfillment in love, for Amanda is thirty-five. Her figure "pathetically slender," her blond hair "painstakingly crimped," her eyes "anxious blue," and her expression "something deprecating,"

Amanda had sacrificed her days without complaint to the comfort of her loved ones and to "the desire of peace and good-will [that] had crept into her face and stayed there."[30] Even though Caleb has been visiting Amanda every Saturday night for fifteen years and although voluble Aunt Melissa threatens to speak to him about his intentions, Amanda wishes nothing said to him. Her wait-for-tomorrow philosophy has sustained her through nursing one sick relative after another, and now she lovingly cares for her aged and ailing mother whose wits are gone—a calamity Amanda refuses to recognize as she continues to treat her mother as if she is purely rational.

Into Amanda's self-sacrificing and uncomplained-about life comes a tricky Yankee buyer of old goods who, in the brief absence of Amanda, manages to trick Amanda's mother out of an antique eight-day clock and some handmade quilts. When Amanda returns to her mother's belated distress over the loss of her possessions, Amanda literally steals back the heirlooms her mother has unwittingly sold for a pittance; and in her unaccustomed aggressiveness and departure from decorum and peace, she wins the proposal from Caleb that had been denied her for so many years.

The very real courage of Amanda is only hinted when she lays the little roll of bills the stranger had given her mother at his dinner plate, but "her cheeks were scarlet, her thin hair flying."[31] The overcoming of the inertia of habit and pride because of another represents an account of love in its finest expression; for the obedient, timid, docile Amanda becomes quite a different creature under the stimulus of this love— a creature so different that Caleb, seeing her "wheelin' that great thing all alone"[32] (the eight-day clock in the wheelbarrow) overcomes his own shyness and pops the long-awaited question. The "Righteous Bargain" is double-barreled: the stranger has his money back, and Amanda's mother has her precious heirlooms; but more important, Amanda and Caleb have each traded natural reticence and inertia for an unaccustomed outward show of emotion when compelled to act not for self but for a loved one. Amanda's self-forgetfullness in her mother's cause has brought a great, though unexpected, reward.

Thus *Meadow-Grass*, dedicated to "M.G.R.,"[33] Lover of woods and field and sea," insists on an orderly world of right-thinking, right-living, deep-caring inhabitants. The wrongdoer finds either help to the path of righteousness or to payment in kind. The life is hard; the rewards are few; but an underlying contentment sees life whole and insists on a genuine capacity for service of one person to another. When an elderly relative ails, his kin tenderly cares for him; when trouble comes, a neighbor holds out his hand. Communion, the final end of love, is present in the very real concern of man for his neighbor. And the concern aids toward the communion.

The stories in *Meadow-Grass* find their setting in Tiverton. Additional stories of the New England people of this town continue in Miss Brown's next published volume of short stories, *Tiverton Tales*, in which she continues to explore values by taking a long view of existence, by insisting that life is not an end in itself, and by standing on a spiritual foundation; in so doing, she may come closer to a true perspective than would be possible with the introspective narrow view based upon one person's empirical experience, so often the subject of modern storytellers. As Peter Berger has observed, "In openness to the signals of transcendence the true proportions of our experience are rediscovered. . . . This in no way implies a remoteness from the moral challenges of the moment but rather the most careful attention to each human gesture that we encounter or that we may be called upon to perform in the everyday dramas of human life."[34] In *Tiverton Tales*, more consciously than the other collections of stories, Miss Brown attempts this perspective, not only by viewing individual lives in the light of eternity, but also in selecting for focus actions that give insight into human character for the betterment of human relationships.

"Dooryards," which opens *Tiverton Tales*, presents in vignette country people such as Della, the wife of a farmer who never smiled. Della, who improvised a croquet set by using withers for wickets, apples for balls, and a clothes-slice for a mallet, played her game in solitary joy; for "although loneliness begins in pain, by and by, perhaps, it creates its own species of sad and shy content." Della did not live to old age, which was of some relief to those "who were not altogether satisfied with her outlook here";[35] but Della, while she did live, joyfully used her croquet game to compensate for her otherwise joyless life.

Miss Nancy's dooryard, a "travelling garden," mirrors Miss Nancy herself, "victim of a love of change; for "no sooner does a green thing get safely rooted than Miss Nancy snatches it up and sets it elsewhere," so that her front yard becomes a "varying pageant of plants in all stages of misfortune." But Miss Nancy's lack of luck with plants reflects her "fierce impatience against the sluggishness of life. . . . She hurries her plants into motion because she herself must halt";[36] for Miss Nancy cares for a peevish, bedridden father. A farmer who trades useless articles for more useless articles has a yard that swarms with young life, as children adventure happily through the discards. In describing the dooryards, Miss Brown compels the reader not only to visualize the variety of appearances but also to probe imaginatively the reasons for their differences; for in the differences lies an insight into the working out of frustrations into an acceptance of what one cannot change into what one can endure with some satisfaction.

"The End of All Living," which closes *Tiverton Tales*, describes the Tiverton cemetery and, of course, the people who once inhabited Tiverton. A spirit of joy rather than sorrow pervades the information given about these former inhabitants, and even the grave of a "purple flower of a maid" reminds Miss Brown that, although one might feel that the earth is poorer for her loss, such is really not so "since the world holds other greater worlds as well. Elsewhere she may have grown to age and stature; but here she lives yet in beauteous permanence, as true a. part of youth and joy and rapture as the immortal figures on the Grecian Urn."[37] The tombstones, evidence of the dead as the dooryards are evidence of the living, manage to bring to life again those who lie under them; and the stories that lie between the opening and closing essays represent the meeting of life and death, for Miss Brown's characters act not only in the light of their present conflict, but also in the full knowledge of the day of eternity. An acceptance of the oneness of life and death becomes the focal point of many of these stories as the illusory present fades in the knowledge of a greater reality.

"Horn O' the Moon" tells the story of Mary Dunbar, who although born in Tiverton, gave up her home to go to the poorer community of Horn O' the Moon to nurse people; for Mary, born for service, cannot see a fellow creature in need without aiding him. Into her life, and needing her service, comes ill Johnnie Veasey, who, full of tales from the seas he has just returned from, opens for Mary the enchantment of faraway places that were only pictures in her old geography. But Mary nurses Johnnie back to health and into the arms of a girl he had left behind at South Port. When Johnnie sends her three gold coins instead of the proposal of marriage that might have been expected, Mary feels "not the poorer for what her soul desired; she was infinitely the richer, and she remembered the girl at South Port, not with the pang that once afflicted her heart, but with a warm, outrushing sense of womanly sympathy"[38] as she vows to keep the gold coins for her burial.

Even though "Horn O' the Moon" might be considered a tale of unrequited love, Mary has become part of the mainstream of life. Knowing that her service and her sacrifice in nursing Johnnie back to health have sent him to another girl, Mary rests secure in the knowledge that her life has counted for another in the way she remained unable to make it count for herself. Life for a human being does not consist merely of what happens to him, but, far more important for the inhabitants of Tiverton, of what one has caused or helped to happen to others. The satisfaction of knowing that one lives a good and purposeful life is not limited to personal gain or personal happiness but represents a knowledge that humankind is inexplicitly bound together in common destiny.

A deeper exploration into the mysterious relationship between human beings, and between human beings and a larger reality, manifests itself in "A Last Assembling," a story which attempts to image existence itself. Dilly Joyce, "born into such willing harmony with natural laws, that this in itself seemed to belong to her life," has waited for fifteen years, while taking care of aged relatives, for Jethro Moore to return from the city where he had gone to seek his fortune. At the story's opening, Dilly has just buried the last of her relatives and must sell the old homestead to pay a dead brother's debts; and she at last finds herself free to marry Jethro. She must now pack up the few family treasures she can afford to keep before auctioning off the rest, an ordeal she dreads, because although people feel that a human means very little to Dilly, "that was not true. It was only true that she held herself remote from personal intimacies; but all the fine, invisible bonds of race and family took hold of her like irresistible factors, and welded her to the universe anew."[39]

As Dilly walks to the old homestead to carry out her dreaded task, never in her life has she seen "less of the outward garment of things." She is "dumb to the beautiful outer world," but "broad awake to human souls; the souls of the Joyces, alive so long before her and stretching back into an unknown past." She feels faint misgivings over her task, realizing that she must "lower the curtain" and "sweep them from the stage."[40] While engaged in her tasks and while poring over the family treasures, she is surprised by Jethro, who paints what is to him a delightful, but to her a threatening, picture of what city life will hold for her—cars going by her door, maids to do her work. Suddenly she feels queer, almost afraid of the new life beckoning to her; but she feels at the same time that her ancestors stand around, ready to help, although what help they bring remains vague to her. But that night she secretly flees from her bedroom at a neighbor's home and sits in the old homestead.

And the ancestors "come" to Dilly as she sits throughout the night in the family homestead, and Dilly understands their "souls" bound somehow to the old house, which had "called on her to come."[41] As she thinks about these men and women from whom she herself was descended, she thinks of the shoemaker who had gone off wildly to the woods at the news of the Battle of Lexington and who had drowned himself after three days and become the family disgrace. Now he stands here: "Was it the man, or some secret intelligence of him? . . . and Dilly out of all his

race, was the one to comprehend him." And Dilly understands that he was torn between his conviction of the
wickedness of killing and his desire to help his country;
therefore, he "chose the death of the body rather than sin
against the soul. And Dilly was glad; the blood in her own
veins ran purer for his sake."[42]

When Dilly remembers Old Delilah Joyce, left on her
wedding day, to waste away for love, Dilly sees her without the pathetic bravery of her wedding gown and knows
her for a woman "serene and glad." Then Dilly thinks of
Annette Joyce who, to the disgust of her kin, had clung to
her husband through one debauch after another and had
gained for herself only the mockery of those who had felt
her sense of decency must be lacking. But now, on this one
night, Dilly knows that Annette's life had been a "continual laying hold of Eternal Being, not for herself, but for
the creature she loved; that she had shown the insolence
and audacity of a thousand spirits in one, besieging high
heaven and crying in the ear of God." Somehow, Dilly
knows now that Annette was "of those who overcome."[43]

As Dilly sits through the long night, she becomes aware
of souls of whom she had never heard; and she knows that,
"faulty as their deeds might be, they had striven, and the
strife was not in vain. She felt herself to be one drop in a
mighty river, flowing into the water which is the sum of
life; and she was content to be absorbed in that great
stream." She feels the "safety of the universe" as she smiles
"lovingly over the preciousness of all its homely ways."
She also sees "how the great chain of things is held by such
slender links, and how there is nothing that is not most
sacred and most good. The hum of summer life outside the
window seemed to her the life in her own veins, and she
knew that nothing dwells apart from anything else, and
that, whether we wot it or not, we are of one blood."[44]

As the ties that her ancestors hold become apparent to her,
Dilly also becomes aware of herself; and in this awareness
dwells the recognition that Jethro also was an inheritor and
that it was not he but his inheritance that she loved. Because
he now foregoes his inheritance, she must forego him; for
she rests secure in the knowledge that what had been be-

tween them, although good, was not what they had thought it to be. Although something fine and beautiful leaves with Jethro, she cannot mourn; for "the Joyces had done their work, and she was doing hers."[45]

Although this story might appear on the surface to be based on the conflict between the pull of the beloved and familiar against the strange and innovative, more depth appears. One of the ancestors, indeed, was willing to stick beyond all human expectation to the one she loved—apparently one who had not denied his inheritance. Alice Brown hints in this story about love which, in the true mating of two people, transcends the physical and the emotional to enter the realm of the spiritual. It is this truth which Dilly's ancestors have revealed to her in an unconscious warning that failure to be true to her "inheritance" would result in failure to be true to herself.

In addition, Dilly learns that a way of life in itself can be rewarding. Society tends to pity the spinster, certainly the New England spinster, with no regard to the immense rewards that may be realized from service to others. To understand "A Last Assembling," one must go beyond the provincialism of society's view to stand on a height not only to view a whole life, and become aware of the present, but also to glimpse, inexplicably and mystically, the past and future as well, all blending into one whole—an awareness Dilly gained through her fifteen years of nursing one aged relative after the other through a last illness. Dilly has chosen what for her is the greater part; and she has affirmed, in her choosing, the value of life apart from marriage, family, society, wealth—an affirmation built on a strong conviction that principles of steadfastness, courage, love, and service spawn not only like principles, but happiness as well.

Similar to "A Last Assembling," the value of the past to the future forms the underlying theme of "A Second Marriage." Amelia Porter, widowed just a year, sits waiting for the beau she had given up in pique to marry a man twenty years her senior fifteen years before. While waiting for Laurie Morse, her unmarried "true love," Amelia looks around the home which had remained the same as her husband's grandfather had left it, although every other house in the neighborhood had gone from the "consistently good to the prosperously bad" in the matter of furnishings; and she muses on the life she had lived with her quiet, tender, elderly husband—a life lived with deference to him, both for his years and for her having married him without love.

As Amelia looks around, mentally relegating furniture to the attic, Laurie comes calling; but when he attempts to take her in his arms, preparatory to taking up where they had left off fifteen years before, Amelia shrinks from him, feeling a subtle barrier between them. Puzzled, Laurie leaves; and Amelia takes to mending her deceased husband's coat, wishing to have all his clothes in order before laying them aside forever (and hinting to the reader that she cannot bear to part with the memory of her husband). Amelia's Aunt Ann comes to see her; and in mentioning how everything is exactly the same as it always was, Aunt Ann mentions a little still in the attic that her husband used to have such a royal good time with, "makin' essences." She motivates Amelia to bring it down and also a little spinning wheel that her husband had liked her to use, even though other women dropped such work. Amelia sits down to spin, wrapped about by an atmosphere of "remoteness and memory."

When her aunt goes home, Amelia finds that her former loneliness has been transformed into peace: the "worldly voice, strangely clothing her own longings with form and substance, had been stilled; only the clock, rich in the tranquillity of age, clicked on, and the cat stretched herself and curled up again."[46] When Laurie comes again, Amelia refuses to let him hang his coat where it will touch her husband's or to let him sit in her husband's chair. She vehemently tells Laurie that she can't go back "any more than you could turn Sudleigh River, and coax it to run uphill." She doesn't know what has made her a different woman, or "whether 'twas meant my life should make me a different woman; but I *am* different, and such as I am, I'm his woman." And her voice rings with triumph, as if she were taking again an "indissoluble marriage oath." Even though she admits that she had expected all through the years that Laurie would finally come back to her, that she wanted him to come, and that she had planned what their life would be together, Amelia concludes, "I guess I didn't lose by what I've lived through. I guess I gained somethin' I'd sooner give up my life than even lose the memory of."[47]

So Amelia sends away the lover who would have taken her into a new life, fits a roll to the spindle of her spinning wheel, and begins "stepping back and forth as if she moved to the measure of an unheard song, and the pleasant hum of her spinning broke delicately upon the ear. It seemed to waken all the room into new vibrations of life. The clock ticked with an assured peace, as if knowing it marked eternal hours. The flames waved softly upward without their former crackle and sheen; and the moving shadows were gentle and rhythmic ones come to keep the soul company. Amelia felt her thread lovingly. . . . 'I guess I'll dye it blue,' she said, with a tenderness great enough to compass inanimate things. 'He always set by blue, didn't he, puss?' "[48]

Amelia, like Dilly and Mary Dunbar, finds a way of life completely different from the commonly accepted one; and she indicates Alice Brown's insistence on the value of life itself. These heroines, along with Miss Brown's others, are not denigrated because they have neither husband nor children; for their lives are not weighed by pragmatism or practicality. The measure of their lives consists of service to others, inward peace, and fidelity to a life force that flows instinctively through their uneducated selves and makes them one with each other and with all mankind.

Although the focus has been given to theme and psychological insight in *Tiverton Tales*, mention must be made of the homely dialect, the rich folk humor, and the shrewd comments of Miss Brown's New England characters. For example, Amos, Amelia's cousin in "A Second Marriage," who virtually gave up talking while still a youngster, does so only when strictly necessary. Under the prodding of his voluble mother, however, Amos vouchsafes a reason for his taciturnity, thereby offering the perfect squelch: "If one head's open permanent in a house, I guess that fills the bill. . . . I ain't goin' to interfere with nobody else's contract," and his mother looks after him lips gaping, "and for the space of half an hour, spoke no word."[49] Like Amos, all of Miss Brown's characters speak vividly in a dialect that seems an authentic recording; it carries the lilt of the humor and the homely wisdom of those at home—not only in a small town but in the universe.

The County Road—a collection, first published in 1906—reveals a surer form, a tightness of construction, and a greater depth than the previous collections; and the stories attest to Miss Brown's expanding artistry. Among the most interesting ones in this collection, one very often anthologized, is "A Day Off."

Abigail Bennett, wife of Jonathan, a "born meddler" who "interfered for the common good," silently suffers the augmented meddling of Jonathan, when he is housebound because of a broken arm, until his meddling promises to interfere with their daughter's plans to meet her fiancé. Abigail cautions Claribel, her daughter, to slip out without her father's knowing it; for both know that Jonathan will find some excuse for keeping Claribel from her date. Abigail tells her first lie in response to Jonathan's question concerning the type of cake she is making; knowing his thrifty spirit, she tells him it is a one-egg instead of a two-egg cake and then expertly cracks both eggs together. Abigail tells her second lie when she informs her husband that Claribel will not be able to help him as he had expected because she has sent her to a neighbor's.

With the second lie, a "strange exhilaration" possesses Abigail who "did not remember to have lied willfully in all her life before."[50] Her practice was always to tell the bare truth, despite temptation, even though she suffered for it; but now that she has begun to lie, "she liked it." Recklessly enjoying the fabrications, she piles one upon the other in order to countermand the stingy orders of Jonathan. Her aim is to provide generously for Claribel's wedding day and to prevent his selfish meddling from destroying her daughter's youthful joy. Abigail "thought with wonder of the ease with which new worlds could be created merely by the tongue. It gave her a sense of lightness and freedom. She could almost forgive Jonathan for meddling, since he had introduced her to these brilliant possibilities."[51]

Abigail, who continues her day of one lie after another, is

having the time of her life as she purchases, through lies, happiness for her daughter. At the end of the day, she confides in awe to Jonathan that she had found out something momentous, that it "don't do to do the leastest thing that's wrong," not because one might be found out, but because "wrong-doin's so pleasant." The way of the transgressor is not hard; rather, it is "elegant" and "enough to scare ye to death, ye have such a good time in it, an' ye go so fast . . . like slidin' down hill an' the wind at your back." She confesses that she had had a "splendid day . . . best time . . . for years." Even though she tells herself, "I ain't ever goin' to have another like it. I don't dast to. 'Twouldn't take much to land me in jail. But I ain't sorry, an' I ain't a-goin' to say I be."[52] One has the impression that, if necessity requires, Abigail has her own happy remedy for her husband's meddling and may have another "day off."

Aside from the genuine delight in having the meddling farmer receive his comeuppance, one enjoys the lively humor of Abigail's inventiveness. Although Abigail lies for a very fine purpose, she knows that she offends not only against truth but also against wifely obedience; but she also learns that wrongdoing can be very pleasant. Even though the reader becomes aware of her oversimplification, Abigail's conscience defies the stern New England dictates of right and wrong. As she protects her daughter, she stands as a monument to all mothers. Her wisdom and her understanding of her daughter oppose the selfishness, miserliness, interference, and callousness of Jonathan, who would be considered a good man in his society. Abigail's "day off" illustrates that, paradoxically, apparent good and apparent evil interchange; and the way of the transgressor is not hard but pleasant.

All of the mothers who live along the County Road are not so solicitous of their daughters' happiness as Abigail—particularly Mrs. Bourne in "A Winter's Courting," a woman "sworn to rule." Mrs. Bourne rules her daughter, Myra, from the time she has snipped off her daughter's golden hair (after seeing Myra admire it in a mirror) until she has succeeded in breaking off her daughter's engagement. The story opens a year after Anselm, Myra's former fiancé, has gone away and immediately after Mrs. Bourne has left to visit relatives. Myra's first act after her mother's departure reveals the defiance she had hidden since the unfortunate shearing: she loosens the hair which she had worn severely pinned back to forestall another shearing, and she puts on her Sunday dress, ornamenting it with her great-aunt's best fichu, in rebellion against her mother's constant dictum that "beauty is a snare." While relishing her beauty, Myra receives a visitor, her former fiancé Anselm, who, having heard that her mother has departed for the winter, has returned, prosperous and determined, to claim Myra as his bride. Anselm authoritatively tells Myra that the time for minding her mother has now passed; she must now mind him, at least until they live together and learn to "mind each other, turn an' turn about."[53]

Anselm's first order horrifies Myra: she must go with him to Parson True's to get married. In spite of Myra's rather feeble argument that her mother "ain't very strong," Anselm convinces her that her mother's strength far surpasses what Myra's will be if *she* "ain't looked out for"; and he succeeds in getting Myra to make the bargain of giving him just this one winter as his wife; then, when her mother returns, he will agree that she return home, if she wishes, and he will return to his business in the city. Although he agrees with Myra that the bargain he offers is an outlandish one and he remarks that "we ain't so terrible knowin', if we were born in Sudleigh," Anselm is "knowin,'" enough to master Myra, born to take orders as her mother was born to give them; and in "pale obedience," her objections overcome by the determination of Anselm, they marry. However, Myra sees herself through her mother's eyes, and she recalls the day "when she had been guilty before and all her golden hair lay scattered at her feet."[54]

Myra and Anselm live a fairy-tale life during the winter, for Anselm treats Myra like a cherished doll and Myra gaily assumes the chores she had done so obediently for her mother, even to planning a garden, although Myra convinces herself that by spring her new life will end and she will be again taking care of her mother. When her mother finally returns and is accompanied by an ailing sister, Myra has the house ready for her; but the task had been accomplished with tears streaming down her face at the thought of leaving her husband. But as Myra starts to sit down to supper with her mother and her ailing sister, she suddenly blurts out her status as a married woman and declares that she must immediately leave to make her husband's supper. As she does so, she realizes that Anselm and Parson True must also have known she would do as she has because love and a stronger loyalty would break the silver cord, and the domineering mother would have to accept the accomplished act.

The complete docility of Myra becomes plausible against the setting of a community in which such obedience is customary, and the symbolism naturally flowing from Myra's beautiful hair gives psychological credence to the mother-daughter relationship which has not been allowed to follow a normal course. Part of the appeal of the story lies in Myra's gradual awakening to herself as she rebels outwardly, spiritually, and emotionally; but her intellectual rebellion follows only when self is forgotten through love of her husband. Unlike many present-day Myras, Myra Bourne had one chance offered—and she took it; for Anselm, strong in his love, forced the freedom of the timid creature who, unable to loosen her own bonds, would have doomed herself to the sterility of a life of slavery to a domineering mother.

Not all the stories in *The County Road* concern mothers, but all concern the trouble that arises when a loving relationship goes awry, either through selfishness or inattention to the needs of another. In "A Sea Change," Cynthia throws her husband's heavy greased boots out the door; for they represent a "misery borne to the last gasp." At forty, Cynthia is surfeited by her life alongside of the mountain that she longs to climb, yet cannot ever, either literally or symbolically. Although she does her chores and takes care of her husband, she hates him and the life she leads. Symbolically throwing him out of her life with the boots, she informs him that she is going to Penrith to visit her sister Frances; but she does not reveal that she means never to come back. As Timothy, her husband, goes to get their little store of money from a broken-nosed teapot, he takes instead a little china cup, fills it with water, and drinks from it. When he wipes it, he breaks it and remains unconscious of the fact; for "cups might easily fall when worlds were falling too."[55] In that single sentence, Timothy stands, not as a brutal husband, but as a human being flawed by insensitivity; but he is also the victim of a hard and methodical life.

As Cynthia walks to the station where she had taken her trunk the day before, she rehearses her speech to her sister. She would tell her that she couldn't live with Timothy any longer and that she will support herself. When her sister asks why, she will say, "He greases his boots so much. He leaves 'em by the oven door." She can remember nothing more of his faults, but she knows that the reason is sufficient, that "any woman would know."[56] Loving service of long years' duration turned into a mechanical taken-for-granted routine bursts into hatred in Cynthia; for lack of love acknowledged and expressed by a taciturn and overworked husband makes each day a drudgery.

Cynthia's sister lives beside the sea; and lying in the little bedroom that overlooks the sea, Cynthia learns from the doctor that she is "tired out." She is exhausted from cooking, sewing, cleaning; from lack of company; from lack of a vacation; from lack of joy. She looks so old that her sister, who is ten years older, had recognized her only because she wore their mother's cameo brooch. But her sister will care for Cynthia, nourish her, love her, just as she once cared for her own child, now dead, who was not like other children but who had brought her two parents together in a loving relationship that gave focus to their lives, that made them smile and sing happily for her sake, and that brought them together in a love expressed originally for her sake but continued in its own right after her death.

Although Cynthia grows plump and pretty again under the ministrations of her sister and the Cap'n, her husband, she becomes convinced that she is a helpless invalid; she transforms her psychological need into a physical one. Not until her sister feigns illness herself does Cynthia rouse herself from bed and stay out of it. Gradually, she regains her zest for life because of the tender, loving care lavished on her; and hope and joy return her to life under the spell of a sister who is both tutor and model. When Timothy comes unexpectedly one morning for her, Cynthia throws herself in his arms sobbing. "Oh, how good it is! Oc, can't you kiss me? You smell jest like home." Timothy, hair cut and beard trimmed, adapts himself quite readily when she perches on his knee, a position she had seen her sister take with the Cap'n. With keen, new, home-hunger, she asks about the mountain, confessing that she can scarcely wait to see it; but she also insists that Timothy stay for two weeks to have his "change" as she has had hers. Frances and the Cap'n will visit them, and she will show them the mountain. When Timothy asks her whether she meant never to return to him, his eyes are wet; he looks to her like "an unreasoning creature which has suffered pain, and gained a lifetime at a bound." When she answers that she had meant to stay away until she became good and strong, the lesson is learned: Timothy will again love and cherish; Cynthia love and bloom with his cherishing.

Although society no longer demands the back-breaking day-to-day farm chores of most of its women, the underlying problem of tacit acceptance of each wife and husband in an uncommunicative home has not diminished. The delicate interrelationships presented in "A Sea Change" hover gently over a world in which Cynthia had to endure the knowledge that "nobody had put warmly affectionate arms about her for a long time"; and Alice Brown, although she writes again and again of the loving work of a wife for her husband (and vice-versa), strongly insists upon the recognition in love of this service. "A Sea Change" vividly explores outward actions motivated by inner psychological needs. Cross-currents and themes give a greater substance to this story than appears in many of Miss Brown's other stories. With "A Day Off," "A Sea Change" merits a place among the most significant of American short stories because of its artistry and its universal value.

Although almost no children are pictured in Alice Brown's short stories, most of the earlier stories concern themselves with the attitudes and habits of young lovers; however, older, wiser, and more mature parents, relatives, and friends shape their attitudes and habits. The stories in *Country Neighbors*, however, focus for the most part on middle-age, and Alice

Brown herself was fifty-three at the first publication of this collection. Added to the solution of conflicts in these stories, her emphasis affirms a good, benign world, a world of gardens, a world of beauty. These same recognitions and attitudes cause Marietta in "A Poetess in Spring" to express the same faith as David in John Updike's "Pigeon Feathers" when she says, "Course I got faith. . . . I know. . . . I guess it's because the sky is so pretty. . . . Maybe the robins have got something to do with it."[57] In Alice Brown's stories, when resignation becomes necessary because of what one cannot change, a spirit of joy accompanies it. Even though Miss Brown does not use the method of the psychiatrist's couch to probe the "why" of human behavior, she presents accurate insight into such behavior; she solves the hard problems of existence with the "act as if" school of behavior rather than with the "understand why" technique. The problems of her characters are often capable of solution because natural surroundings bear witness to an orderly universe of vast and intricate design that is not only part of but also a model for transient man.

"A Flower in April" illustrates the pictorial quality of Miss Brown's art in presenting a psychological truth about human beings without probing for the whys and wherefores of it. Ellen Withington and her mother live "in a garden." A house behind the garden 'takes secondary place, being merely a place to shelter them during the months when life must diminish to poring over seed catalogs in preparation for their real life of "weeding, tending, transplanting, with an untiring passion." Ellen, herself a flower, has an "apple-bloom face, and violet eyes down-dropped" with gold hair; and she dresses in "soft, sad-colored stuffs rather like the earth."[58] Ellen is perfectly satisfied with the clothes that serve their purpose of keeping her warm or cool as the weather requires; for to her, beauty grows only from the ground. Ellen is satisfied until the world beyond the garden suddenly floods in on her.

Ellen has no intimate friends, for her life is her garden. Unlike other girls her age who "flared their petals to the sun and begged for cherishing," she is "like a bud, all close and green"; but she has been forced to notice all the courting couples, strolling arm and arm past her garden; and when an acquaintance, Susan Long, confides that she herself will soon be wed, Ellen flees to the safety of her garden because she is troubled by her thoughts of the significant and terrifying future she envisions for the couples. But, curiously, something pulls Ellen away from her garden the next day; and she slips over to Susan's, where Susan shows her all the delicate clothing that she will wear as a young bride. Susan then takes her to the homes of the various young unmarried girls where she sees lace, braid, and delicate cloth everywhere. When, later that afternoon, Ellen suggests to her mother that she, also, would like to have beautiful new clothes like other girls, her mother looks at her in wonder— the first inkling that the reader receives that Ellen is "different."

And for weeks, so long that the garden almost runs to weeds that spring, Ellen and her mother stitch lovely dresses from woven cloth from the attic. One Sunday, when Ellen walks to church in a pink and blue silk and wears a hat with pink roses under the brim, her excitement brings a rush of color to her face, eliciting the remark that "Ellen Withington's a beauty." So outwardly changed is she that the minister applauds her return to services, even though she has never missed a Sunday. The next week, when she comes to church in a "foam of white like a pear tree," she inspires one of the young men to sue to take her home; but Ellen clings to her mother's hand, leaving him to dodge their steps all the way home. Safe at home, Ellen, still holding her mother's hand, entreats her, "I needn't ever be with anybody but you, need I?"; and her mother reassures her that she need not.

A few days later, Ellen is overtaken while walking home from the store by Milton, Susan's intended husband; and too timid to refuse, she allows him to give her a ride in his wagon. In answer to his attempts to make conversation, she admits that she has made many pretty things like the other girls; and her confusion adding to her beauty, he attempts to kiss her. But she flies out of the wagon, "like a bird let loose from an imprisoning hand"; and in spite of his apologies, she trembles until he has gone. That evening, when her mother informs her that a young man intends to call on her later that evening, the same young man who wished to see her home from church, Ellen implores her mother to entertain him. The mother and the young man converse about crops together in the parlor while Ellen remains "safe" in her garden weeding a bed of pansies. One pansy, "quite human in its sombre wistfulness," causes Ellen to kneel and kiss it; for she knows that this is the "only sort of kiss she should ever want to give."[59]

A psychological interpretation of this story might tempt one to attribute Ellen's lack of attraction to the opposite sex to the fact that no mention is made of a father figure in her life or to the fact that her mother does not wish to give her up; but these ideas are not even faintly suggested by Miss Brown. Ellen's mother appears loving and caring; her only fault, perhaps, is not pushing her daughter toward marriage, but she is perfectly willing to help her achieve it if she so desires. Miss Brown, who insists on the individuality that does not cater to mores, finds once more that the worth of a woman is not intrinsically tied to her marital status. The many happy spinsters and widows in Miss Brown's stories exalt life from a woman's point of view and bear out the finding of present-day psychologists that, in general, single women may indeed be happier than married women. Ellen, described in the imagery of her beloved garden, will, like Candide, find happiness in cultivating her garden.

The effects of maintaining close relationships with the beauty of growing things appear also in "Gardener Jim." Since Jim cannot bear to see a garden unattended, he takes care of all the gardens in the neighborhood entirely without recompense, purely for the love of the growing things in them. He buys his simple needs with money earned from making shoes in the winter; his tending the gardens of others emphasizes the fact that he has no garden of his own. Years before, his wife had run off with another man; and Gardener Jim, attempting to wipe out every trace of his life with her, had ploughed up the garden she had loved, had sown it with grass instead of flowers, and had thrown out all the housekeeping items not absolutely needed. As a result, he now keeps house in a primitive setting and spends the warm days tending the gardens of others.

Because gardens have become his special province, Jim notices that Annie Darling's garden, in her absence, needs attention. Annie holds a special place in Jim's heart, for she had been going with his nephew, Wilfred, who, in Annie's absence, has been seeing a newcomer. Gardener Jim succeeds not only in getting Wilfred to tend Annie's garden but also pointing out the folly of Wilfred's behavior with the newcomer. As Jim tells his nephew, 'There's a time for everything. There's a time to graft a tree an' a time to cut it down. Well, it's your time o' life to make a 'tarnal fool o' yourself. Don't ye do it. If you do, like's not when you're my age you'll be all soul alone like me, an' goin' round 'tendin' to other folk's gardins.'[60] As Wilfred tends the garden, which is so much a part of Annie Darling, he realizes that she indeed must be his "darling Annie" and that, when she returns home, she will return both to a beautiful garden and a true love.

Gardener Jim not only succeeds in preventing Wilfred from making a fatal mistake but brings together the Miller twins—two elderly spinsters who had not spoken to each other for thirty years, because a man had led both of them on, had caused them to quarrel, and had run away with Gardener Jim's wife. Each sister has her own half of the house, just as each has her own garden. Through the apparent innocent meddling of Gardener Jim in such mundane occupations as taking down the rotting dividing fence and attempting to cut down a tree which had been planted by the sisters' mother, the sisters make remarks to each other; and the story concludes with Gardener Jim's telling Wilfred that the Miller twins are going to have flapjacks together for supper and with his telling Annie that she shall have the set of flowered china that had belonged to his mother.

The story has overtones symbolized by the gardening that has become the mainspring of Gardener Jim's life. Gardener Jim, the instrument for bringing Wilfred and Annie together and for settling the anger between the Miller twins, himself attains healing. Just as he had let his own garden go, he had let his life go; through his own deep hurt, no longer loved. As the gardens grew over with weeds, unattended, their owners suffered from the lack of love which made life pass by in sterility. But Jim's saving grace, the habit of gardening, sustained him, so that although he did not enter again the human mainstream of love, he kept the sluices open. He began to care about Annie Darling and the Miller sisters; and through his efforts on their behalf, he made himself again into a whole human being, as evidenced by his giving his china to Annie. The deep hurt heals when he opens himself to others.

Obstinacy of another sort appears in "The Other Mrs. Dill." Although Alice Brown would not regard herself a feminist in the modern meaning of the term, she does recognize the inequality of women in a man's world. Like Abigail in "A Day Off" who had to lie to attain her daughter's happiness, Mrs. Dill must resort to trickery to override the obstinacy of her husband. Myron Dill has decided to uproot his wife from their homestead of thirty years to move her to a new home in spite of the fact that Mrs. Dill knows that the new home should go to their son. Hermie has been his father's unpaid hired man long past the time when he should have formed a family of his own. In spite of his wife's argument that the new home belongs as much to her as to him and that she should have some say about it, Myron is adamant. Used to having arguments with and then obedience from his wife, he vociferously proclaims that she must not set her will in place of his.

The arguments become more heated, for Mrs. Dill fights for a son against a husband/father who is as stubborn as he is short-sighted. Denying that she must have her own way, Mrs. Dill blames her own stubbornness on her "double personality," which, she tells her husband, insists she's a fool to do what she feels is not right just because her husband tells her to do it. When Myron attributes her strange argumentative behavior to tiredness or need of a change, she assures him that she can do nothing with her "other" personality, that it's getting the best of her, that "other creatur'" that wants to have its own way. It's been growin' and growin' same as a child grows up and now it's goin' to take its course. Same's Hermie's growed up, you know. He's old enough to have his way, and lead his life same's we've led ours, and we've got to stand one side and let him do it."[61] As Mrs. Dill removes the blame for her cantankerousness from her will to her "other personality," she can maintain the arguments on an objective level to which her husband cannot very well object—she has a scapegoat for the digs with which she prods him.

When Myron remains firm, refusing to entertain even for a moment his wife's suggestions that they are perfectly happy where they are and the new home must be for their son, Mrs. Dill allows her "other" personality to dominate; and this personality insists that he must sit with her, neglecting his chores the while, in order that he might make "it" go away. She assures him that, if left alone, she might even set fire to the other place, or draw her money out of the bank and give it to her son. Finally, she feels herself overpowered by "that terrible creatur' inside of me," and he must "stand from under."[62]

In desperation at ever being able to reach him, Mrs. Dill, still playing her role of "the other," calls Hermie in and tells him the new home is his; but his father's expression is so forbidding that Hermie replies that he refuses to go against his father's wishes. Myron, however, worn down by his wife's behavior and belatedly remembering his own father's proclamation of freedom for him, gives Hermie his hand saying, "It's my own will, Hermie." The story closes with Mrs. Dill back at the stove fixing dinner—once more the subservient, obedient wife.

The plot, like that of "A Day Off," turns on the tricking of a somewhat stupid husband by a quick-witted wife who, despite her superior intelligence and sensitivity, is doomed always to laud and obey her husband as lord and master. Perhaps Miss Brown registers a gentle protest about the way things are accepted in a society of male supremacy.[63] But in spite of Miss Brown's apparent acceptance of subservient roles for her heroines, she recognizes the strong individual, be he male or female; for society, not nature, causes the inequality.

Thus, in these collections, Alice Brown's men and women live their lives as individuals; they accept or deny the conventional way; but they always live in accordance with the rule of love in a world in which each individual has a right to choose. As Amelia "moves to the measure of an unheard song," so does Dilly, the village witch, rich in wisdom and understanding because she has chosen the single path in full knowledge of her destiny. So also does Mary Dunbar, who finds her worth, as well as her happiness, in service to others; Ellen Withington, the flower born to blush unseen, blossoms, spends her love on nature's beauties. Again, Abigail, Myra Bourne, Cynthia, and Mrs. Dill must rebel against a stifling code of obedience to parent or husband to make themselves into complete persons. Gardener Jim sustains life through love of his gardens, and these gardens reward him not only with their loveliness but with their aid in cementing broken human relationships. In all cases, rebellion or acquiescence freely chosen diminishes frustration and allows sanity to prevail. Plain people and common clay have indeed yielded to Alice Brown their treasure.

II *Mystical Tales and Parables*

Although Alice Brown justifiably receives critical acclaim for her New England tales, two other types of short stories must be mentioned: the first, stories which do not necessarily focus on New England mores but are mystical tales that attempt a probing of the world beyond the physical one— stories that explore through parapsychology the communication possible through mystical union; the second, parables, many of which lie still unpublished in the Yale University library.

High Noon, a collection of mystical tales, was reprinted in 1970 in the Short Story Index Reprint Series by Books for Libraries Press. Charles Miner Thompson finds, in these stories, a more conscious literary technique than in previous collections of Alice Brown's stories, but he also finds a false lyricism for which he blames Miss Brown's ideas on love— ideas based on the emphasis that loving, like virtue, should be its own reward, ideas preached over and over again.[64] Although his criticism has some justification, the preaching does not always flaw the story. The reader sees Rosamund mature through experiencing pain in "Rosamund in Heaven"; he sees the destructive force of jealousy in "Natalie Blayne"; he notes redemption through suffering in "His Enemy," as the doctor's striving parallels that of Katherine Anne Porter's Granny Weatherall, for "he might have answered that, had she not laid his former life in ruins, he never would have been this kind of man."[65]

The stories in this collection also contain many shrewd critical comments, such as, "Life is the true thing and art is the garment. . . . Sometimes we aren't born with enough insight to keep on translating the things of God or seeing the world as it really is."[66] And Edith, in castigating the writer John Stafford for his prostitution of talent, might be speaking to much present-day talent when she says: " 'You are emptily cynical, epigrammatically mischievous over the homely, sweet, wholesome things of life. You are the darling of fashionable women, who pout over your abuse of their sex, make pretty wry faces, and then swallow all you say. You are the victim of fine dinners and the elaboration of civilized life. You have foresworn the patience to do the things which must be done prayerfully; you are willing to be fantastic in order to appear great. You are cultivating the vice of clever speaking and the affectation of believing in nothing and nobody—*because it pays.*' "[67] Such lyricism is not false.

Another theme in this collection that reveals lyricism based in truth concerns the defiance of death by love. In "A Meeting in the Market Place," John Stafford finds his mate only when she dies, as he "seemed to himself not so much oppressed by tragedy and loss, as distinctly enriched through them. . . . He saw into the vista of time. His soul ranged herself on the side of obedience. He had inherited."[68] What he had inherited was a vision of a life untrammeled by the earthly restrictions of time, place, and corporality, an experience to sustain the insidious corruption of the flesh until such time as the spirit, untrammeled at last, might find its haven. A parallel exists between today and the early twentieth century, when pragmatism and progress soured and when ideas cut down old ideals but did not produce new ones.

One story in *High Noon* which strikes a particularly relevant note is "The Book of Love," a story which, in probing the psychological differences between men and women, emphasizes how such differences result in lack of communication. In this story Elinor takes over the task of helping John Graham finish an anthology because of the illness of his sister Sally. Falling in love with Elinor, John, who calls her a "reasonable" woman, tells her that she "could lead a man's life, all work and no play."[69] Elinor attempts to give him some insight into a woman's heart, as she makes up a story and tells him that "the woman was made to live in a House of Love, where two creatures together build up something imperishable. I mean something out of the spirit of life, which is more real than life itself. But the man didn't know there was such a house, and the woman had to live in it alone."[70] The man and the woman are, of course, John and Elinor; but because of John's lack of sensitivity to her feelings, she is undecided about how the story should end. She thinks she should kill the woman by having her drown in a storm at the seashore, thereby paralleling her own death of love in conflict, a contemplated ending she makes known to John and Sally.

The resolution of the story comes after an especially stormy time in which the sea has been roaring for three days, causing John sleepless nights, for Elinor has gone back to town and the storm echoes his own inner turmoil. On the third evening, called by an unseen presence, he strides along the sandy road to the beach under a bright moon: "The moon was regnant in a crystal sky. In that flooding splendor he felt alone as he had never felt before. The rote of the sea called to him and made him the more desolate. He was bereft, undone, in a universe once filled with life, but now darkly hostile to him. He knew at last what seemed to him the wrong of being: to have been made to run inexorably in one narrow groove. . . ."[71] But at the shore, he sees Elinor, who having been called to the roaring sea by a letter from Sally, has come for the atmosphere needed to kill her heroine; and she has silently "called" him. Instead of killing her heroine (herself), Elinor will let her live, as she herself will live in a House of Love which, although not the harbor of the idealistic love of her immaturity, will shelter the "reasonable" woman she has become.

The compromise has been effected by both Elinor and John. Elinor (presented as a sermonizing idealist) and John (pictured as an unimaginative pragmatist) represent the failure caused by alienation. One member of the romantic partnership finds it impossible to appreciate the ideals of the other: Elinor expects an emotional peak in a love-centered life; John expects a prosaic plain in a work-centered world. Even though deeply in love, Elinor admits, "We live together, yet really we each live alone. It terrifies me."[72] Such a situation has been terrifying novelists ever since, particularly those who do not employ characters with imagination enough to experience their partner's plight and respond to it. Elinor and John have both experienced and responded; John has learned of the spirit, while Elinor has learned of the flesh.

Another story in this collection of mystical love stories is "Rosamund in Heaven," which treats of the now-popular theme of adolescent growth through confrontation with the hard facts of existence. Rosamund, an adolescent, is struck forcibly by a preacher's words that "heaven is within us."[73] In love with life and its beauties, and in love with a man fifteen years her senior, she attempts to communicate these "heavenly" feelings to her mother; and she wonders at the splendor of her feelings as she takes great delight in her youth, her beauty, and her love. As she reproaches her mother for never having told her that heaven was within, her mother answers: "I can't tell you things till you get to them. You wouldn't hear me if I did. I suppose there are exquisite overtones, this minute, in these summer sounds; yet we are both quite dull to them."[74] Rosamund is forced, then, to experience growing pains of unrequited love as well as to gain a glimpse into the sordid suffering life of another in order to find that her own heaven existed only in childish illusion, that life in its deepest experience is knowing and suffering the pain of existence; and Rosamund truly, though not so dramatically, learns the message of the Book of Job.

As Miss Brown attempts to bring the "overtones" of life and love to those who are "quite dull to them," she presents the emotional side of man with mystical overtones as a better guide to reality than the intellectual side—a creed that the poet, at least, must applaud and that the scientist, at last, must investigate. But as Miss Brown probes psychologically the many needs of man, she flaws the stories by filling them too richly with truths made too explicit, thereby stereotyping her characters. Even though the slight plot entertains, the stories appear too pat, too well-made; but they do promise greater artistry in later stories since flashes of wit relieve the serious discussions of life and love as man and woman become antagonists in their fight for a common ground upon which to build a life.

Charles Miner Thompson's criticism that the message is preached over and over again has validity, but it is the preachment rather than the message which causes the falsity of tone, when such appears; for certainly a love and virtue that require reward result in neither love nor virtue. Therefore, as a vehicle for Miss Brown's ideas, as a probing into the mystical and psychological meaning of the man-woman relationship, these stories succeed. As a slice-of-life, as a mirror held to reality, they disappoint, primarily because of stilted dialogue in which characters pour forth poetic phrases that expound Miss Brown's ideas but leave the reader outside of the struggle, the conflict, and the high ecstasy that is talked about rather than imaged.

In an unpublished letter to the Reverend Joseph Mary Lelen on April 10, 1931, Miss Brown wrote: "I already know that 'God created man for happiness' and . . . I believe we *could* have it on this earth if we could *wear through* our present ignorance of His laws and His will, and help Him make His Heaven."[75] This attempt to wear through ignorance underlies all the stories. As a Unitarian Humanist schooled in Classicism and Christianity, Miss Brown attempted to sort the wheat from the chaff; but as an artist, she formed the piles a bit too neatly in these stories, leaving it to greater artists to present life in its complexities instead of its simplicities. Recognizing her own flaw, she also wrote to the Reverend Lelen: "I have no 'associative memory' as Professor Lowes says about the Masters, Shakespeare, Milton, Coleridge. I am a small intelligence bumbling alone—like a bee and drunk on beauty."[76] But although Alice Brown denies herself an "associative memory," like that of the "Masters," she interprets the world to men. She finds in her interpretation a benign and happy universe in which the ills that men bear stem from their failure to properly equate their actions with eternal good.

A review of *High Noon* in *The Nation* states that these stories should be read singly, that in the bulk they seem precious, seeming to represent the eternal feminine "tiptoeing down the ages, her own soul in her hand, searching for new quintessences of herself." But read singly, they fill one with an "almost breathless perception of the writer's clear vision into human relations, a vision that sees straight and around corners as well." Calling Alice Brown the "Mary Wilkins of the superfine emotions," the reviewer admits that she "dries her weeping pages with a dash of bright, warm humor," and what there is of morbidity comes from the "eternal ladies" themselves.[77] The humor of those who lack a sense of humor is presented particularly in these stories, and Alice Brown pricks many a bubble of self-complacency, but she does so with an irony that is gentle and a wit that is subtle. The vivisection of wedded and soon-to-be-wedded love sheds no blood, and wounds heal quickly and completely; and even though the reader may not be startled into agitation, he may well be delighted into reflection. The mystical stories deserve further attention, as do the parables.

Although Alice Brown wrote many parables, most of them lie, as already noted, among her unpublished manuscripts in the Yale collection. They have never been published as a collection, and they remain, therefore, even less known than her other stories. One, however, a long short-story, published separately, as *The Day of His Youth* (1897), illustrates her imaginative use of this genre. The mysticism of this tale, as well as its theme, bear comparison to Thornton Wilder's works. Thornton Wilder may very well have been influenced by Alice Brown's stories, even subconsciously; for he admits to an acquaintance with them and says, "I remember reading stories of Alice Brown with pleasure. My mother called my attention to them and we would share our successive appreciations." He also states that he associated her "with Sarah Orne Jewett and Margaret Deland—if she was a little less delicate than the first, she was far above the sentimental clichés of the last. And she seemed never to fall below her own sound high level."[78]

The Day of His Youth concerns a soul that seeks love and finds it only after tragedy, when the soul matures to the elevation of a Christ-like love for humanity, thereby leaving its selfish past to unite with the souls of all men. Francis Hume, reared as a scholarly hermit by his grief-stricken father after the death of a beloved wife, falls in love with a cynical, worldly woman who jilts him. When he migrates to the city in search of his own identity and of some sophistication, he despises the poor and the unfortunate he finds there; but he ends by loving them and sharing their pain. But he can share pain only because he himself has felt it; then only does it become real:

And it rushed over me suddenly how they must ache and suffer and languish to be so poor and so ignorant and so vile. There is a dropping inside my heart, all the time, as if the blood that ought to nourish me were falling and falling and wasting itself in pain. And I began to look into the faces, and it seemed to me as if these people, too, were all of them bleeding. The ground was red and soaked. And then I learned that all this great world is in pain just like my own. I did not seem so much alone then—not quite. They were like me, all of them. I began to see how some might love them; and the more hideous they were, so much the more could one love. *Who was Jesus Christ?*[79]

The successful search for the brotherhood of man ends in tragedy when Francis Hume sacrifices his life to save a drowning dog. In experiencing the pain of the unfortunate, Francis Hume has found his soul; and the worth of his sacrifice does not depend on its result but in its self-forgetfulness. Thornton Wilder's theme in *The Eighth Day* parallels that of Alice Brown's in *The Day of His Youth.*

The Day of His Youth consists of an exchange of letters, for the most part, and this technique enables Miss Brown to

probe the depths of innocence awakening into self-aware-
ness as father instructs son and as lover instructs an innocent beloved. The life of Francis Hume is the parable of the
soul's search for itself. For Alice Brown, as for Francis
Hume, the quest ends in a brotherhood of love that has experienced a brotherhood of pain.

The Day of His Youth, one of the earliest of Alice Brown's
works, finds it echoes in many of her later novels. Life as a
quest for soul to be found in brotherhood with its accompanying self-abdication never moved far from her vision. Although *The Day of His Youth* grows tedious through many
pages of sermonizing and moralizing, the importance of its
underlying theme should not be underemphasized. The
theme, however, receives finer artistic handling in Miss
Brown's later works, particularly in the novels; but her ever-
present desire to "wear through" man's ignorance of God's
law constantly hovers menacingly, resulting at times in an
emphasis on philosophical ideas rather than in verbal
imagery.

CHAPTER *3*

The Lure of Broadway

W HEN recalling the thrill of rehearsing her play for
Broadway, Alice Brown described her feeling as "one
big splendor of a moment," for to her plays remained "the
top-most button on fortune's cap."[1] True to her New England heritage, the play she sent for consideration for the Winthrop Ames award of ten-thousand dollars for the best play
to be submitted anonymously by an American author took
its roots from the climate, both literally and figuratively, of
New England. After judging almost seventeen hundred
manuscripts, Augustus Thomas, Adolph Klauber, and Winthrop Ames selected Alice Brown's *Children of Earth, A
Play of New England*, as the most notable in both theme and
characterization. In a newspaper interview after the prize
was announced, Alice Brown responded to a question concerning the anonymity of the judging by remarking that
some of the wildest statements had been made concerning
suggestions that she had written the play along lines suggested by Mr. Ames and that, although there was not a word
of truth in it, it did put her in such an embarrassing position that, when her friends were reading the press notices
aloud, she put her fingers in her ears. When the interviewer
rose to go with words expressing his desire to see the play
when produced, Alice Brown answered earnestly, "And I
do hope . . . that you will like it."[2]

I Children of Earth

But not enough people liked *Children of Earth* to warrant
its success on Broadway. Produced on January 12, 1915, by
Mr. Ames at the Booth Theatre in New York, the play opened

to mixed reviews. *The Boston Transcript* called it a play "rooted deep and branching in American life and character as the New England folk exemplify them and written with a force and ardor of controlled imagination that has transfused into all Miss Brown's insight, invention and processes, the reality and illusion essential in the theatre."[3] *The New York Tribune*, echoing the *Transcript*, called the play "a page from the truly native life of the nation, magnificently written" and stated that the author brought into the lives and characters "a ring of truth that is far deeper than photographic realism, a something resulting from keen insight into the New England heart struggling with a broadly human and vital problem."[4] The reviewer in *The Dial* was moved to say, "apple trees and larkspur and lilacs in bloom, shimmering gowns and rose-trimmed bonnets of an olden time, sap mounting, and everything breaking bounds because of springtime and love in New England."[5] The *Times*, although it considered the story unconvincing, noted that its most conspicuous quality was "its admirable fidelity in atmosphere and spirit to its New England background."[6]

Even though the reviews were mixed, the play caused a stir in dramatic circles. As the *Evening Sun* remarked ten days later, "This play and production have proved so unique that they have caused endless critical and other discussion as to their certain significance in American theatricals."[7] Burns Mantle praised Effie Shannon's creation of the spinster heroine as one that must be "numbered with the notable characterizations of this season."[8] The *Telegraph* of January 26, 1915, which called the play a great one, pointed out that the critics had failed to emphasize the characterization, that Mary Ellen and Peter Hale would suit Aristotle as protagonists, that the characters were like the people of Euripides' plays in strength and simplicity.

While a Saugerties manufacturer was asking Winthrop Ames to serve apple cider in the tearoom of the Booth Theatre at the intermission of *Children of Earth*,[9] one scene of which is laid in an apple orchard, a discussion of the play was being planned by Maurice V. Samuels, secretary of the Society of American Dramatists and Composers,[10] in the Washington Avenue Branch of the New York Public Library

on February 5. The play made an impact, certainly, contro-
versial though the final estimate remained. But Broadway
closed "its eyes and its ears to it," and Alice Brown learned
suddenly "for good and all that doors are not always to be
swung wide, and that sometimes, when they seem to be, one
is only caught in them disastrously, and that if you write
books and plays there is only one happiness you can expect:
that of the hourly enchantment of the writing itself, for then
you are living in your dream."[11]

One of the reasons for the adverse criticism was voiced by
Louis Sherman in the *Evening Globe* of January 23, 1915,
when he admitted that he and others did not like the play
because it was full of the feeling and ideals of New England
that the rest of America resented. He called it "grotesque
masquerading in serious guise."[12] This honesty should be
noted, for it is important to remember that lack of honesty
often led to denigration of Miss Brown's talent and mini-
mized the recognition of the authenticity of the ideals presented when such ideals were distasteful.

Although the play most certainly would appear unsophis-
ticated to a Broadway audience today, it must be remembered that Eugene O'Neill had not yet transformed the American theater. Had he done so, the earth-given values and
the heredity-shaped destinies of *Children of Earth* might
have engaged an audience with its inventiveness; its
brooding, fateful atmosphere of the New England scene; and
its insistence upon the importance of the land, particularly
the Hales' love for Mill Road Farm. Indeed, these qualities
prefigure, to some extent, O'Neill's *Desire Under the Elms*.

Children of Earth, which is set in a small New England
town in the last part of the nineteenth century, presents
Aaron Barstow, fifty-two, hard-featured, sharp, masterful,
and his charming daughter Anita, who, however, reveals
a streak of hardness caused by the necessity of revolting
against the values of her father. Both have returned to the
old colonial farmhouse to take Mary Ellen, Aaron's sister,
home to live with them after the death of their father. Mary
Ellen had been left to care for her father when Aaron left for
the city to make his fortune; and over the years, Aaron had
directed her to buy land in order for Aaron to make himself a

monument in the town in which he was born. Mill Road Farm, a parcel owned by Nathan Buell, Mary Ellen's former sweetheart, must be secured by Aaron in order to complete his holdings. Fortunately for Aaron's plan, Nathan Buell is now coming home after twenty years' separation from Mary Ellen to claim her for his bride now that her father and his objections to Nathan have been buried.

To further complicate matters, Peter Hale, who is Mary Ellen's age, also wants Mill Road Farm, his family's home for generations, which was lost because the Hales were so unmaterialistic that they "always did manage to turn their neighbor's grindstones faster'n their own."[13] The Barstows and the Hales represent opposing forces: the Barstows, attempting to make money, have made life joyless and austere; the Hales have made life joyful and free. The Hales' grandfather, relying on nature's bounty, was called "Old Apple Hale" because he was so "crazed about apples" that he would plant an apple seed wherever he went. Another Hale, even though he had produced a plum with a stone no bigger than a pea, "didn't know enough to get it on the market." Finally, Peter Hale and his nephew, Adam, an agricultural chemist, wished to restore the farm and build it into productivity. The Hales were "always tryin' to git something out o' the earth, somethin' besides money," and it made their place homey and pleasant, perhaps because "folks lived there that enjoyed themselves an' wanted other folks to."[14] The Barstows, rigid and unflinching in matters of duty and industry, required an austerity in living that made their home sterile and unattractive. If Aaron Barstow had ever had an interest in anything besides making money, it had been stamped out by his father, who, in Aaron's boyhood had "ordered him home from Mill Farm,"[15] thereby separating him from the ancestral home of the Hales and, presumably, their love for nature rather than money.

As the play opens, the death of the father and his subsequent burial have recently occurred, releasing the bondage of Mary Ellen. Mary Ellen cannot mourn her father, for she has, over the years, "dumbly fought down in herself every emotion that rebels against the recognized system of things."[16] She can now marry the returning Nathan Buell

even though her brother, Aaron, objects to the union. But
Peter Hale, unbeknown to Mary Ellen, loves her, although
married to Jane, an alcoholic, whose Portuguese origin
makes her an outsider in the straight-laced New England
community. Even though Mary Ellen finally recognizes her
own love for Peter, consents to run away with him, and
spends the night in the woods with him preparatory to
leaving on the morning train, she finds her strict upbringing
too strong for such a revolt and refuses to go at the last
minute.

Curiously, Jane Hale saves Mary Ellen from scandal. As
Aaron is safely headed back to the city, Peter Hale holds
possession of Mill Road Farm, and Anita and Adam Hale
verge on discovery of their mutual love, Jane reveals her
strength in an unconventional decision, as she says to Mary
Ellen at the play's conclusion: "Do you know what I want? I
didn't know last night, but I know now. To have you two
back ag'in. You stay right here in this house an' let me stay
with you. An' we'll work. An' you'll keep the devil out o' me.
An' Peter Hale'll come here an' eat. An' I'll see to the house
down there. An' that's all."[17] And she kisses Mary Ellen's
hand—the hand of the woman who almost ran away with her
husband—in complete self-renunciation and love.

In many ways, Jane reveals herself to be the most interesting character in the play because she broods mysteriously
and her personality is beset by its own devils. Although, like
many of Alice Brown's heroines, she likes to roam the woods
at night to find some freedom, she goes further by abandon-
ing herself to wild singing and dancing, apparently releasing
the torment of the frustration repressed by day. Also, her
attraction to Mary Ellen and her devoted service to her
appear to be founded on a peculiar love. Although not made
explicit, and although Miss Brown's conventional heroines
hold themselves to heterosexual love, Alice Brown evidently
considered such a relationship valid and within the norms
of morality.[18]

To support this view, which does result in Jane's being a
many-sided character rather than a type, the relationship
between husband and wife can be cited: they have been
"dead" to each other for years; no children have come from

the marriage, rather unusual in a farming community; no explanation appears for Jane's addiction to alcohol. Thus the conjecture of psychological problems attendant upon her inability to love her husband—her inability to have children, and her alienation from a community which considers her "odd"—appears valid. Jane's unhappiness manifests itself in a desire to take her own life; her uniqueness resides in her unconventional reaction to the knowledge of Peter's love for Mary Ellen; and her great desire to live with and to serve Mary Ellen finds its impetus in love for Mary Ellen, not in love for Peter. She, along with Mary Ellen and Peter, must "make the best of things."

Of lesser interest as a character, although of greater interest in her role in the plot, is Mary Ellen. Mary Ellen, the obvious heroine, is dominated by a father who kept her in dark clothes and who treated her to his silence for long years after preventing her from marrying Nathan Buell. Her story is the tragedy of a life of repression finally given its chance, only to have this chance refused and resulting in a greater gain. Although Mary Ellen knows no explicit reasons for her father's objections to Nathan Buell, it can be conjectured from his repression of Mary Ellen that they were selfish ones, even though the grasping nature of Nathan Buell, later revealed through his avid desire for the land, rather than the love of Mary Ellen, validate the father's objections.

Forced, therefore, to live with a domineering, selfish father who stifled every breath of personality in her, Mary Ellen took refuge in illusion; she held in her heart the romantic idea of a great lost love as compensation for the sterility of her existence. This meek acceptance of the yoke resulted in her failure to reach maturity; for, feeding over the years on illusion, she could not distinguish between it and reality until, faced with an illusion too immense for her to fit into her scheme of things—the illusion that she could "set back the clock" and thus build a life of happiness on the desertion of Peter's wife—she gains a glimpse of reality and does the right thing.

Peter Hale, also a type who never quite comes to life, is the typical man of the soil, a lover of nature, a dreamer of self-effacing dreams, an idealist who attempts to erase time and space. His challenge is to make things grow where they never grew before, and this includes the dry soil of Mary Ellen's repressed desires. Although his love for Mary Ellen has sustained him throughout his life, the suddenness with which this love is revealed, offered, and accepted verges on the implausible. Aaron Barstow, like Peter a type, presents a direct contrast to Peter (as also does Nathan Buell: both are "citified" country boys) in his materialistic view that money-making is the goal of living. Aaron, having left his home at twenty-one and "got into rubber," hates to remember how he began; and he hates people who remember it, even though he wishes now to provide a library and an iron fence around the graveyard, thus partaking both of life and death.

Anita Barstow, who has suffered from her father's ruthless pursuit of money, reveals that she has "no place" because, out of loyalty and love, she hasn't been willing to "run" with people that wouldn't accept her father. However, she recognizes his shortcomings; and cynical and worldly, she accepts outwardly her father's values, which with young and clear-eyed vision, she understands as false ones. Thus a dominant father who has not provided love for his son and daughter has ruined two lives and bids fair to ruin a third, his grandchild Anita's; for Anita exhibits traits that combine those of her father and of Mary Ellen, her aunt. The inferiority that has been bred into Aaron by his father's dominance has colored Anita's life, so that now she must have the baubles of material prosperity to compensate for the lack of a valid sense of her own worth; the loyalty that Mary Ellen had retained stubbornly for her father finds its echo in Anita's willingness to accept her father's values and conform to them, even though aware of their implications. So alike are Anita and Mary Ellen in appearance that Nate Buell mistakes Anita for the Mary Ellen he had left twenty years earlier. With an inevitability of event, however, Anita is spared the frustration of her immaturity; for had Mary Ellen not suffered the repression afforded her by her father, the daring act of spending the night with Peter would not have transpired—an act that permits Anita to see life in its proper perspective. She now understands the self-betrayal implicit in unquestioning loyalty to a parent's values. She sees Adam in a new light, realizing that her love for him must supersede her loyalty to her father.

The characters of *Children of Earth* draw their sustenance from nature. Although not worldly successes, the Hales represent the strong, the good, the moral people. Even weak Mary Ellen, love-starved throughout the years, finds in the beauty of the natural scene something to feed her hungers. Only those who leave the tilling of the soil to better their fortune in the city become rapacious and evil: Aaron Barstow and Anita attempt to substitute their lack of self-worth for earthly possessions; Nathan Buell reveals his insensitivity and greed almost in caricature. And only when Anita accepts Adam, the natural man, does happiness begin for her.

Swift dialogue, natural for the most part, moves the play rapidly from action to action. Even under the tragic notes, an underlying optimism transfers the drama from tragedy to comedy, as the ending testifies.[19] If the implausible note is struck, as previously noted, it exists in the too-pat relationship between Peter and Mary Ellen, which makes for a well-plotted, rather than a penetrating, drama. In spite of beautiful scenery and poetic language, the play appears to suffer dramatically from an overabundance of plot, resulting in conflicts that must be sensed through reflection rather than experienced through participation. Insight and verbal talent are readily perceived, but the intricacies of plot seem too contrived for dramatic acceptance. The flaw might be that Miss Brown attempts too much; instead of focusing on a central character, she brings in too many lives and attempts to explain them all. This technique works better in her novels, although in them too this apparent overabundance of idea results at times in lack of dramatic presentation. In the novels, multiplicity might be excused; in the drama, it cannot be.

These criticisms made, naturally, after reading the play instead of witnessing it performed, appear valid in the light of Miss Brown's success with one-act plays (the same conjecture might be made concerning the success of the short stories over the novels), three of which had previously been performed with some success: *The Web* at the Bijou Dream in Boston, *Joint Owners in Spain* at the Toy Theatre, and

Mella's Tramp in Pennsylvania by Cornelia Otis Skinner.[20]
Whatever the total reason for the lack of success of *Children
of Earth*, it soon closed and has never been revived.

II   *One-act Plays*

Although *The Web, Joint Owners in Spain*, and *Mella's
Tramp*, as well as other of Miss Brown's one-act plays, enjoyed
production by Little Theatre groups, these plays did not
appear in print until 1921, when the collection *One Act
Plays* was published. Most of the plays in this collection
suffer from melodramatic intensity and from the flaws apparent in *Children of Earth, A Play of New England:* a
too-neat handling of character; a too-well-constructed plot,
suitable perhaps to Little Theatre because of rapid action
and dialogue; and a too-explicit moral. For instance, Millie
of *Millie Dear* discovers that her husband has been accusing
his best friend of the very crime he himself has committed:
the betrayal and the desertion of a young girl. The much-
maligned friend, who suffered heroically for Millie's sake,
is completely vindicated; and Millie leaves her deceitful
husband forever.

In *The Web* coincidences pile up in interlacing incidents
to entangle the characters in events which, when unraveled,
reveal how the first false step has led to an inexorable conclusion. Conway, a former thief, now turned minister, leads
two thieves not only to friendship with the law but also to
the paths of moral righteousness. Conway, having left his
wife and daughter after embezzling a large sum of money,
spends his life trying to pay back the theft. Led to repentance
by his guilt feelings, he now preaches in a tabernacle; but he
is unaware that the tabernacle had been built by his wife
and that his daughter, now married, has become one of his
fervent followers.

Complications arise when Conway's daughter, unaware of
the identity of her father, sends Wellfleet, her husband, to
Conway for help; for Wellfleet has also embezzled from the
same firm that Conway did and has decided to run away—
exactly as Conway had done many years before. Although
Wellfleet agrees to see the minister at his wife's pleading,

he cynically informs Conway that he knows his true identity and that he had embezzled exactly as he himself has. As Conway reveals his anguish over his original deed and its present consequences, consequences attendant upon his running away in the first place, he receives another blow when his companion-helper, whom he has trusted implicitly, reveals that he has considered Conway a fraud all along—has considered him a milker of credulous followers whom he would squeeze dry in one final attempt, the results of which they would both share.

The daughter, however, originally wronged by her father's desertion, shows herself the moral product of that desertion and resolves the conflict. Having listened to her father's sermons, she has absorbed his goodness as he has led her along the path to righteousness. Revealing her trust in him, she convinces her father that he must confess his past error and atone for it. Wellfleet, inspired in turn by Conway's courage when "the threads were broken" but God had made him "keep on weaving,"[21] indicates that he also will confess and take his punishment. The once-cynical companion feels that "religion can't be so rotten after all, not if it makes you a dead game sport. I'm glad I've got it, damned glad"[22]; and the play ends with all threads tied and with Conway's saying, "We'll break bread together. It will be our Sacrament."[23]

Like *Millie Dear* and *The Web*, all but one of the other plays in the collection rather too explicitly point their moral. For instance, in *The Loving Cup* a doctor gives the cup presented to him by his grateful patients on his seventy-fifth birthday to the couple who have quarreled on their first wedding anniversary. The situation gives him the opportunity to make a little speech on loving, cherishing, and being kinder to each other. In *The Sugar House*, a wife saves her husband's sweetheart from a tar and feathering and thereby wins back his love, although the working out of the problems and the problems themselves hold the interest. Some of these plays might still create interest as presentations of Little Theatre groups, but one play in the collection is a gem, perhaps even more timely today than when first produced. The great number of times this play was produced caused Alice Brown to confess that it bought, if not all her bread, the "butter and jam."[24]

This play, *Joint Owners in Spain*, becomes at once an example of village people Miss Brown had known in the flesh[25] and an example of her accurate assessment of the needs of the human personality. A little masterpiece, it might stand as a memorial to her talent as a playwright. It is set in an old ladies' home—a room containing two beds, two chairs, two washstands, and two chests. The action opens with Mrs. Mitchell, director of the home, transferring a delicate old lady to another room because Miss Dyer, "meagre, lachrymose, always injured and looking for trouble,"[26] has worn out her roommate as she has worn out every other woman who had shared the room with her. When Miss Dyer complains that her lot is always to remain in the same room, never being given a better location, Mrs. Mitchell tells her frankly that everyone had accepted that she was cantankerous and had to be borne with, that every roommate had stood it just as long as possible until they were "worn out," but that something will now be done about her; for there are just two in the Home who are impossible to live with—"you and Mrs. Blair." Although Miss Dyer admits that Mirandy Blair would thwart even "the serap'im round the Throne" in efforts to get along with her, she adds that she and Mrs. Blair "ain't no more alike than chalk's like cheese." Mrs. Mitchell agrees with this assessment, but she reveals that, in desperation over her apparent inability to solve the problem, she has decided to make roommates of the two worst dispositions in the Home, different though they are—Mrs. Blair capable, robust, overbearing, and high spirited; and Miss Dyer, sniffly, weak, injured-innocence, and complaining.

After the move is effected, Miss Dyer whimpers about her grievances, her constant upset in the reshuffling of her belongings; and Mrs. Blair berates her for her continual crying and complaining. After much squabbling between the pair— both strong-willed—Mrs. Blair hits upon the scheme of dividing the room in half with a piece of chalk so that each occupant can have her own "home" and a respected privacy.

Miss Dyer, overpowered by the vivacity of her new room-mate and interested in the new game, learns the rules. Mrs. Blair instructs Miss Dyer that the chalk mark represents the partition; that she has given Miss Dyer the morning sun, for she herself would "jest as soon live by a taller candle" in a place of her own; that the chalk line goes right into the closet; and that Miss Dyer "don't dast speak a word" to her unless she comes and knocks first on her headboard, which represents the front door.

As the two old ladies visit with each other, each respects meticulously the privacy of the other by means of the rules pertaining to the imagined partition. They continue their pretense in the presence of Mrs. Mitchell, who gains the insight to exclaim emphatically, "If there's ever a chance for this Home to be divided into single rooms . . ."[27] With their own bit of territory secured, the two old ladies become the best of friends: Mrs. Blair expresses solicitude for Miss Dyer; and Miss Dyer saves the situation when Mrs. Blair forgets to be stopped by the imagined partition by saying, "Here, Mis' Blair, you come right through my house, an' save a step. My! Ain't this grand!" And the two ladies gaily exit together on their way to an outing.

With authentic dialogue and perceptive characterization, *Joint Owners in Spain* rings true with the querulousness, the hurt, and the subdued anger of the old who no longer have a place to call their own and who are blamed for their reactions to an uncaring world. As Alice Brown captures the interplay between these two distinct personalities, she does so with wit and humor; for not one note of sentimentality or pathos appears. These ladies demand respect as individuals, in spite of their poverty; most of all, in spite of their faults. And on the deepest level, the solving of a human problem by means of consideration and love shows no boundaries of age or of time. The attention demanded of each for the other in adhering to the rules of the game changes the focus of each's attention from the faults of the other to the impersonal. With a common goal (maintaining the separation of living quarters), as well as a real sense of having a spot of earth for one's own, the two old ladies supply to each other the love,

the acceptance, and the privacy lacking in an institution-
alized existence. For this play, if for no other, Alice Brown
deserves the title "playwright."

II *Other Dramas*

Another play that should have special mention is *Charles
Lamb*, a five-act play published in 1924 but never produced.
Edwin Clark, reviewing it in *The New York Times*, remarked
that Miss Brown's ten-page introduction to the play disarmed
criticism, for she cited the enormous difficulties involved in
trying to bring to life Charles Lamb, as well as Samuel Taylor
Coleridge and William Hazlitt. With stilted dialogue, the
characterizations border on parody, reminiscent of the " 'Way
Down East' genre of drama."[28] Faced with an enormous bulk
of material about Lamb, Miss Brown focused on "not
chronicling the weather that beat upon Charles Lamb and
his beloved Mary, but the stoutness of heart with which they
met it."[29]

The play mentions, rather than dramatizes, Charles
Lamb's devotion to his sister; for it is filled, for the most part,
with poetic dialogue between Charles Lamb and his illus-
trious acquaintances; and even though Miss Brown indicates
that Lamb has sacrificed everything for Mary, the depth of
his devotion never grips the reader. At the play's end, as
Lamb muses, content with his memories of the lover he had
refused, he represents a long line of Miss Brown's heroes
and heroines, beginning with Julie in *Kings End*, who find
their strength in renunciation and their excellence in courage to serve the beloved.

One last play, *Pilgrim's Progress*, privately printed in
1944, should be briefly considered because it is Alice
Brown's last work and because it summarizes her view of
life as a pilgrimage which, part of a larger journey, attains
completion only after its earthly span of years—the view to
which all of her themes may be reduced on the most fundamental level. Like John Bunyan, she was Christian on the
way to the Celestial City; and although the way was fraught
with danger and suffering, the help of others and her own
faith in the goodness of life and the certainty of the Kingdom
in the Sky[30] at the end of the journey made the progress a

happy one. For Alice Brown, a life lived with courage and hope surmounts the very real evil in existence; for through evil, good stands revealed; through suffering, wisdom is attained: the vision combines both the tragic and the Christian.

Pilgrim's Progress, a drama in five acts, purports to tell the events leading to John Bunyan's writing of his *Pilgrim's Progress* and to present Bunyan's story in dramatic form. At the start of the dream, which is the fifth act and the part of her play based on Bunyan's *Pilgrim's Progress*, Miss Brown notes: "Though the *Pilgrim's Progress* was at least begun during Bunyan's imprisonment in Bedford jail, even if not completed there, we may surely allow ourselves to put its date a trifle earlier. For so may we not only serve the drama, which is the interplay of life, but take all possible advantage of a certain vivid phase in historic England. Also the conversion of Christian's wife, Christiana, has been dovetailed into his arrival at the celestial city, because affectionate minds have sometimes suffered over his seeming desertion of her on earth, while he stormed his way to Heaven, where, as it proved, they were again to be united in their love and worship."[31]

The play opens with Otway, who, in love with Bunyan's wife Mary, is apparently successful in his desire to get rid of Bunyan by sending him to London to warn Parliament that the dethroned Charles II is on his way there to attempt to rally support for himself. Bunyan's reward will be five hundred pounds, a fortune that can be used to succor his blind child. Instead of taking the journey to London, however, Bunyan rides toward Worcester to warn the king instead, because Christ has made him "to believe no man, king or cowherd, should die by treachery."[32] Bunyan also voices Miss Brown's own sentiments: "This rich bloom of earth—how it bewilders and beckons us! 'Tis not so much that heaven is far away. The earth itself is heaven. . . ."[33]

In gratitude to Bunyan, the king, prompted by the gypsy Meg Finch, with whom Bunyan has had a romantic encounter, later sends gold to Bunyan who is in prison because he has insisted upon preaching whenever he wished to do so, despite the laws against such unorthodoxy. When Meg

Finch comes to visit Bunyan in prison, declares her great love for him, and asks him to run away with her in an escape she will contrive, he sends her away; but she has left him something that is "better than gold and more enduring. Memory. Seeing her, I have thought back over the years. It is a long time and now life seems to me a path leading from birth to death. And looking back on it, I can see that, however confused we are on the path, and mayhap think we have lost our way, 'tis the straight path we must follow—straight—straight."[34]

After the visit is Bunyan's dream, the dramatic re-creation by Alice Brown of parts of his *Pilgrim's Progress*, with the exceptions noted above. The play ends with Christian's calling to his wife, "(calling softly, as if he had learned new certainties completing what must be) Christiana! Christiana! Come! Oh, Come!" Alice Brown ends her writing career at age eighty-seven with a renewed acknowledgment that, for her, the ideal relationship between a man and a woman is inextricably connected with the soul's journey through this life to the afterlife. From a hint in her letters to her close friend the Reverend Joseph Mary Lelen, one suspects that she has merged with her heroines and with the pilgrim Christian as she, with soaring soul, calls to the Reverend Lelen, her ideal love, "Come. Oh, Come!"

Although *Pilgrim's Progress* reveals stereotyped characterization and a banal situation, the implausible love that Meg Finch avows for Bunyan shows a marked similarity to the like but implausible love of Miss Brown for the Reverend Lelen; they are both part of, perhaps, the same yearning toward the spiritual that is exemplified by the gypsy's attraction to the minister and by the unorthodox believer's attraction to the priest. Despite Miss Brown's failure to come to grips in the play with any mental and physical suffering connected with the beliefs for which Bunyan, the nonconformist, went to jail, despite the lack of any real conflict, the play arouses interest; but it does so primarily because it affords insight into its author's ideas and creed—ideas and creed on which she built not only an extremely successful writing career but apparently an extremely contented life as well.

Except for *Joint Owners in Spain*, therefore, Miss Brown as a dramatist stands on a lower rung of the ladder of literature than that reached with her short stories and novels. Her novels move her a giant step higher.

CHAPTER 4

The Complete Life—The Novels

" "ALL we who crowd to warm ourselves before your fire
. . ." is Josephine Preston Peabody's poetic tribute to
her friend, and it might represent not only the acceptance of
Alice Brown's view of reality by the men and women who
formed her circle of friends and literary acquaintances but
also a general acceptance of Victorian optimism that view
contains. This optimism, like Tennyson's, viewed man's
moral nature as being in an evolutionary process and man's
spiritual nature as giving evidence that the material universe must be controlled through moral laws. The hope,
even the conviction, so prominent in the works of Alice
Brown that, as noted previously, man must wear through
man's ignorance of God's law[1] to find his way in a universe
completely benevolent is a great distance from much present-
day conviction that suffering cannot be justified—one that
creates anxiety and anguish for those not at ease in the universe.

Although Victorian optimism has suffered denigration as
an unreal vision, Milton long before "knew how very much
the issues of human happiness and misery must depend on
the kind of universe man believes himself to inhabit—whether he finds it benevolent, malevolent or merely indifferent. But that it is a supremely benevolent universe is for
Milton virtually all that man needs to have revealed in order
to lead his life rightly."[2] In addition to agreeing with Milton,
Alice Brown presents in her novels plans that point the way
to right living through understanding not only the ways of
God but also those of man. By imaging lives which "wear
through man's ignorance" (or society's conventions) to find

the main flow of eternal verity, she shows not only the order of the universe but also the beauty of its design.

Irene Samuels believes that the "implications of Milton's cosmic scheme come prophetically close to the thought of Teilhard de Chardin."[3] She finds that both Milton and Dante Alighieri (although Milton more than Dante) regard the world as being what men make it; and for both "we make it better if we acknowledge our dependent relation to the totality of things."[4] Since Alice Brown's vision embraces that of all three, the warmth that Josephine Preston Peabody and others find before the fire of Alice Brown consists of a poetic vision, which, like that of Milton, Dante, and Chardin, embraces the natural and the spiritual in one unity and which acknowledges man's relation to the totality of things.

Not surprisingly, Miss Brown finds Robert Frost, also, a kindred spirit; early in his career, in 1915, just after the publication of his American edition of *North of Boston,* she wrote: "He is a scholar, and yet he has not allowed himself to be unduly moulded by the great original. Therefore he has lost nothing of his unique genius—which is the expression of New England."[5] She also praises Frost's faithfulness to the New England atmosphere and nature: he "finds meaning through experience in New England but that meaning is not purely local; he speaks of the individual yet universal concerns of man's role in the world and of the spiritual and physical demands made upon him."[6] So also does Alice Brown, who, born and bred in New England, is the product also of the greatest of poetic visions; and the knowledge of what she knows intimately fuses with what she sees imaginatively, thereby lending to her novels the scope that lifts them above the provincial and into the universal.

The emphasis on the universal problem of man in relation to the spiritual, emotional, and physical demands made upon him lends Miss Brown's novels the moral complexities that she (like Henry James and Edith Wharton) feels to be the only proper background for fiction. Although her protagonists in general, like Alice Brown herself, find themselves at home in the universe, psychological assaults on personality caused by selfishness, greed, and lack of wisdom lead such characters to aberrations that result in unhappiness and that may ultimately lead to tragedy. However, the Victorian idealism that patterned itself on a fundamentally good and benignly designed universe forms the frame of reference against which her characters move.

Some of the broad themes that underlie the novels are explorations into love and creativity, the problem of evil, man-made conventions in conflict with natural good, and the conflict between desire and duty. With precision of event as well as characterization, Miss Brown moves her characters from conflict to solution. Although her later novels reveal a questioning that her earlier ones lack, all of the conflicts stem from man's inability to see the good before him and his failure to act according to a fundamental moral order. Miss Brown lived long enough to question; she did not live long enough to doubt. Even in her ninety-first year, courage and hope informed her life, just as courage and hope had informed her novels throughout a long and successful writing career.

I *Love and Creativity*

My Love and I (1912) and *Margaret Warrener* (1901) both explore situations in which love, creativity, or both are thwarted. Revealing the plight of the lover or of the artist, Alice Brown shows the impossibility of attaining the ideal of each in a world less than ideal. However, even though compromises must be made, these compromises do not lead to frustration but to increased productivity—either to love or to perform artistically. For love and creativity, mutually exclusive, give impetus in the sublimation of one to a heightened awareness of the other.

My Love and I stands midway in the period of Alice Brown's greatest creativity; and although some of her other novels surpass it in art and in plausibility, it clearly demonstrates the places of love and creativity in her novels. Written in the first person, *My Love and I* takes on the dimension of a narrator—in some ways similar to F. Scott Fitzgerald's Nick Carraway—who, both intrigued and repelled as he grows from ignorance to knowledge, if not wisdom, owes his life to an author who in many ways is himself. In the novel, Martin Redfield, a writer, describes his life up to the point at which a reconciliation with it has been made; and he begins the telling in Dickensian phrases: "I was born in England, of the ordinary self-respecting farmer and his wife, and I unlike them was urged from the beginning of conscious life, by the desire to advance, to go somewhere that is not here, to know something that is not this, and to do unproven things, all probably included in the phrase my mother used when she presented the case to my father; 'make something' of myself."[7]

Early orphaned, Martin must make his hard way with menial work; but befriended by an English gentleman, Mr. Egerton Sims, he receives education and polish, although of an old-fashioned variety, as Sims's secretary. The high point of his education is learning of the relationship between the body and the soul, for he learns that the "tyranny of the one must never threaten the mastery of the other," since, in the decent man, there is "no divided house . . . no secret chambers."[8] The influence, though strong, ends early; for Sims dies in his sleep. Martin, again thrust into the world, becomes a hack writer; and he lives at Aunt Cely's boardinghouse and frequents the "Toasted Cheese," an impromptu club of misfit artists. Among these are a painter who has a color theory but cannot draw; a musician who has a guitar but cannot play; a poet who writes, but only prose; and John Blake, the poet who writes poems but cannot sustain the physical demands of life. Blake, who believes that every man must "take his own line,"[9] helps Martin become a sustenance-earning writer, if not a good one.

Martin marries the "Ivory Maid," Mildred; but when he naïvely pictured her as the ideal of womanhood, he failed to assess her correctly as a materialistic social climber. When she insists on a socially higher and increasingly expensive life, Martin, forced to prostitute his talent to produce false and sentimental potboilers to pay the rent and the luxuries, falls in love with Ellen Tracy, truly an ideal woman. Ellen surrenders him rather than have him become soiled by a failure to live up to his own ideals, just as Mary Owen, the subservient healer of hurting humanity, refuses to marry John Blake, although desperately in love with him, because she realizes John does not return her love on the idealized level. Martin makes his peace with himself, with his talent, and with his world as the novel closes with his acceptance of the compromise existence offers.

The value of the novel does not lie primarily in the growing awareness of Martin, although his development lends interest as he gradually changes from a jaunty, rather cynical young man to a more thoughtful, more mature man who has accepted his niche in the world without resentment and is willing to "take his own line." The major value lies in the exploration of the paradoxical in life as it pertains to love and creativity. Both, according to Alice Brown, carry with them enormous gains balanced by enormous losses. Martin, although he accepts willingly enough the labor required to maintain his wife in luxury, always remains detached from the luxury that his labor has purchased; and he laments secretly the prostitution of the talent such labor demands of him. Only when a suspected former lover attempts to pay for his wife's luxuries does he reach, through his injured ego, the decision to cut his standard of living and compromise with his life by attempting to do his best work while, at the same time, supporting his wife and child.

As Martin grows in maturity, he recognizes a need for his wife—not the rapturous need he feels for Ellen Tracy, but the fidelity of commitment to promises. Because he notes the tear-stained face of Ellen at her aunt's funeral, he comes home with "eyes opened to the secrets of other faces . . . and heart all warm to give ease to other hearts,"[10] and he can offer his wife the "tender compassion that responds to every call, the world-sorrow that wakes at sight of the world-pain."[11] Thus Martin settles for the middle course: the writing of literature that is good but not great; the living of a love that is adequate but not ecstatic. On both counts he will be content, if not completely happy; and like Alice Brown herself, he will use his talent "for writing out the lives of individual men and women, a little talent, perhaps a serviceable one."[12]

In contrast to Martin, John Blake settles for nothing less than the highest ideal, even though willing, because of his compassion for overworked Mary Owen who worships him, to lower his poetic sights to encompass the earning of a living in marriage to Mary. Mary, however, will not accept the sacrifice; and even though Blake receives no material reward, although such reward would have been great had he allowed his play to be sentimentalized, he stands as a monumental human being who spends himself physically and artistically in poverty and hardship but who lives life to the fullest because he has made no compromise with existence.

Just as Martin cannot attain John Blake's vision and the fire of creativity, neither can he realize in actuality the rhapsody and the imagined ecstasy of the love idealized through a psychic meeting with Ellen; for Martin and Ellen "meet" in an Eden of happiness beyond the physical universe. But Blake cannot attain the perfect joy of this imagined Eden because, even though he loves Ellen, Ellen loves Martin. For Alice Brown, perfect beauty, truth, and love exist beyond attainment of earthly man; and although the search for each carries with it nonfulfillment, hope remains that one day a new existence will open to the heart's desire.

Blake believes that "all life throws off life by the energy of its being" and that humanity insanely has "woven a veil for the face of nature and so cut itself off from the apprehension of God" by fabricating a scheme of religion, politics, and social ethics that drew it from God.[13] And poetry, to Blake, dwells in heaven; but sometimes she "curves nearer us, a few of her pinions drop, now and then, weighted with our grime—the smoke of our chimneys where we make things to keep our insides muddy—these pinions flutter down to us and we snatch at them and stick them in our caps. But we no more see Poetry as she is in the skyey regions where, a maid in her Father's house, she wanders at her happy tasks, than we see the soul clamped into a gross body."[14]

This Platonic vision encompasses both creativity and love: both exist ideally in another state; both can be but glimpsed in momentary reflection by mortal man. Although man cannot reach either ideal, he has a choice. He can compromise, as Martin does, taking the prudent way, living the dutiful, the good life; and, in its living, he may make it

easier for the noncompromiser, such as Blake. Blake, march-
ing to a more subtle tune, spends himself physically in the
attempt to bring a glimpse of immortality—through poetry
that no one buys—to the compromiser. Idealized love, impossible of attainment also, receives recognition by
both Ellen Tracy and Mary Owen, who are miles apart in
education, wealth, and beauty; for each makes the supreme
sacrifice for the beloved. Ellen insists on an uncompromising fidelity to duty from the admittedly old-fashioned
Martin; Mary insists on an unwavering loyalty to love from
the tortured genius Blake. Neither puts her own happiness
first because each knows, irrevocably, that such self-seeking
would destroy not only the ideal, but the beloved as well.

Yet, even Mildred, cold, self-aggrandizing, and social-
climbing, aids in Martin's maturing; for Martin himself
causes part, if not all, of his predicament. Allowing himself
to be overwhelmed by Mildred's beauty, he marries her
after only six meetings; and he has been able "to put nothing
in his wife's face and draw nothing out."[15] The implication
remains that he has not tried very hard, either before or
after marriage, to engage in the vital communication necessary for the proper building of a marriage. As Martin calls
Mildred "Little Mother" at the end of the novel and as she
responds to his compassion, Mildred appears also as the one
sinned against.

Love and creativity, then, run parallel courses in *My Love
and I;* but as the title indicates that both creativity and Ellen
Tracy might be considered Martin Redfield's "love" and as
the singular indicates that they might be considered to be of
one essence, the difficulty of defining this "love" becomes
apparent. If a psychological definition of love might be
attempted, if love might be described in "very general and
nonscientific terms as the capacity to give spontaneously of
oneself either to people or to a cause or to an idea, instead
of retaining everything for oneself in an egocentric way,"[16]
then creativity might be seen to stem from the same root as
love. In *My Love and I* Alice Brown investigates the connection.

My Love and I emphasizes artistic creativity, which, although parallel to and of the same essence as love, requires

a relinquishment of human bondage in love to survive; but *Margaret Warrener* emphasizes the relinquishment of creativity in a search for the human bondage of love. Margaret Warrener, a gifted actress, makes the complete artistic sacrifice by giving up her successful career to marry Llandaff, a mediocre artist. At the start of the novel, Margaret and Llandaff have just come to live in a rooming house called "Babine," which has taken its name from a Republic of Fools; for the persons who companion one another there are all "remarkable for some ridiculous or imbecile action, or some weird and striking humor" and "have no object save pleasure."[17] Like the "Toasted Cheese" of *My Love and I*, "Babine" members live in frustration: William Deane, young and mediocre, aspires to be a poet; Brandon, a middle-aged reporter, despairs of writing a play; St. John, past his youth but muscular and handsome, wastes his life and his substance attempting to repay a youthful folly; Teresa, a waif nicknamed "The Child," has lost her ability to sing; Laura, most interesting member, insincere and calculating, manipulates people to obtain the utmost in luxury for herself.

Laura, highly intelligent as well as physically splendid, is described in terms of a material earth goddess; and she becomes a goddess to Llandaff. Attempting to sketch her, he falls in love with her; for the love of his wife, Margaret, which is completely self-sacrificing, fails to satisfy the emotionally immature Llandaff who needs to be nurtured by a mother-figure rather than have a wife. But Laura uses Llandaff, as she uses all for her amusement or gain; for to her, love is merely a fever of the blood, enormously ironic, the great joke the powers use to keep mortals prisoner; and she refuses to be bound. Llandaff, who thinks that love goes back before reason and even before birth, surrenders himself completely and unreasoningly to Laura. For Margaret, love remains the great reality; and she always thinks of it with death.

This triangle forms the basis of the story which centers primarily on Margaret's unrequited love for her husband. Brandon, the cynic, watching Margaret's pain unfold before his eyes and, himself wounded through love, finds in Margaret's suffering the impetus to tragedy; and he writes a successful play based on Margaret's agonizing situation. Brandon also loses enough of his cynicism through his love for Teresa, even though St. John wins her in marriage, to attempt another play. But Margaret, who remains the great sufferer, watches the love for which she gave up her own artistic career swept aside in her husband's infatuation with Laura. The climax comes when Margaret learns that Llandaff has an incurable disease. As her pain pales before the agony of learning of his approaching death, she faces reality for the first time; she sublimates her pain, recognizes that love is not "barter, merchandise for money, exchange of give and take"; to love is to "offer all, demanding nothing— that must be love: to give and give, and pour it out as sunshine and the rain come down from heaven."[18]

Margaret hides her agony in the need of her husband; and as she crucifies her love, she endures; for she has substituted devotion and sacrifice as she learns "such a thing in the life of spiritual devotion as an endurance fed on sacrifice."[19] The life force of this spiritualized love surges in Margaret after she attends Teresa's wedding to St. John. Seeing their love, the "pain and beauty of being made so keen a pang that she was breathless under it." Feeling again the "wonder of this thing called life," she reaches forward "eagerly to the next fruit it had to offer her, bitter as it might be."[20]

But bitter indeed is the fruit; for just as Margaret's courage has been revitalized, Brandon comes to her with the news of Llandaff's suicide with the words that "he has escaped." Yet his death brings Margaret closer to her husband than life ever had; for as she sits calmly on the floor with her head against the dead man's breast, "she felt no more alone than he who was dead beside her, only that they both seemed alive and incredibly near each other."[21] Like Ellen Tracy and Martin Redfield in *My Love and I*, Margaret feels her soul fused with Llandaff's beyond earthly mortality.

With her husband's death, the drain on Margaret's creative force has stopped; and she plans to resume her acting career. Called a cocky one, one who never gives up, she agrees that she is; for she considers life to be a "system where you work for pay," and "if you're not paid, somebody is." She resolves to reach artistic heights for Llandaff who could not reach them himself. Her love, flaming, quenched, debilitating, sublimated, spiritualized in turn, now becomes the impetus for her attempt to make her life count for them both. Brandon, constrained by her faith to use the present, says that Llandaff is a very lucky fellow; and Margaret yearningly hopes that he is now a little happier, that some-day they may find happiness together; but if they do not, well, she "will have tried to buy him something, after all."[22]

In the close bond between creativity and love that is the underlying thesis of *Margaret Warrener*, creativity, born here through suffering, comes only after Margaret has ex-perienced the anguish of love unrequited. Only then can she rise to full stature as a dramatic actress; only after Bran-don, sensitive to pain though he is, has suffered Margaret's pain with her can he create a tragedy; only after Teresa has lived through the sickness of relinquishment in vowing to give up St. John can she find her voice. Laura, the uncrea-tive, the unloving, the hard, the insensitive, remains in stag-nant, sterile immaturity; and her final act in the novel is the exploitation for publicity value of Llandaff's suicide. This suicide became possible only through the courage Llandaff received from Margaret's love; and ironically, this suicide, with its attendant publicity, moved the producer to offer Margaret an immediate contract.

Although the giving in love forms the basis for one of Alice Brown's themes in *Margaret Warrener*, more impor-tant, love brings with it its own reward, even though unex-pected and painful. The courage built on Margaret's love for Llandaff stands her in good stead when the loss of this love might have crushed her; and the ideal which forms the courage enables her to turn the pain of rejection into a posi-tive approach to a new life. Far from Philip Roth's cry-babies and John Marquand's neurotics (and far also from those who wallow between), Margaret Warrener walks with the strong heroes of Bernard Malamud and Chaim Potok; she is not, it is true, so memorably etched, but she is impelled to action by the same undaunting moral spirit.

An early reviewer of *Margaret Warrener* calls it a "sex

novel,"[23] but it transcends any explicit theme of sex. Even though the eternal triangle forms the base, the exploration of the giving and receiving in love encompasses the emotional, rather than the physical, reactions of the characters. Miss Brown leaves it to the reader's imagination to supply any and all of the physical details; and like Nathaniel Hawthorne, she explores psychological and emotional depths for which the plot is only the frame. Emphasizing the positive values of love and creativity, Alice Brown finds that both require complete commitment in full maturity; and this maturity, gained primarily through suffering, leads to human growth.

Llandaff, uncreative as an artist and immature as a husband—brought up by "old maid aunts" and then "turned out, with a touch-and-go temperament, into a world he knew nothing about"[24]—feeds on the free gifts of Margaret while seeking the gifts of Laura, the earth goddess (and mother substitute?). Unable to allay his anxiety in creative endeavors, he attempts to substitute pure sensation for fruitful work and emotional commitment. Margaret's emotional demands become excessive when she learns of his defection; and her demands, coupled with her theatrical nature which he has always jealously resented, result in the very action she has tried to prevent—Llandaff's complete rejection of her. Only when she realizes that he is dying can she think of him rather than of herself and loosen the emotional cord, and only when she loosens it can he accept the devotion she offers.

The pain and the apparent inertia of Margaret under the weight of her husband's rejection work through in their own logic as Margaret gradually grows into an awareness of the wholeness of existence in a universe of order, action, and reaction. For even before she has reconciled herself to the loss of her husband's love, she has been able to comfort the waif Teresa, a simple human comforting that stems from an "anguish of sympathy such as they know who are not yet healed themselves." In the very act of affording this comfort, Margaret suddenly understands why she herself has suffered, for she is now part of "the great brotherhood of pain. She was hurt through the hurt of the world, and she could send messages." Impotent in her own suffering, she has learned that "for the keenest pang the gods have medicine" even though the "cup cannot be shared at once" and the tortured soul must "crush its bitter herb and make the potion for itself."[25] Teresa's pain, then, has been the stimulus that provokes Margaret to new insight, just as she can assuage this pain through her own suffering. Pain, for Alice Brown, as for Aeschylus, Euripides, Sophocles—and St. Paul—has a purpose.

Creativity and love, as revealed in *Margaret Warrener*, although growing from the same source, nourish themselves through suffering. Both require full commitment in putting aside the selfish in order that the frustration and pain of an unattained goal transform themselves into a force that propels the individual into a new reality. Then, instead of being crushed by his loss, the lover or the artist uses his anguish to climb to a higher perspective, which shows him service, if not attainment; hope, if not fulfillment; contentment, if not ecstasy.

II *Good and Evil*

On a most fundamental level, the problem of good and evil forms the theme of Alice Brown's writing, just as it forms the basis of writers from Sophocles to Norman Mailer, although a modern writer "because he cherishes so dearly a pinched and starved view of human nature . . . finds himself incapable of rising above sordid misery and achieving the truly tragic vision."[26] Although Louis Bredvold refers in this statement specifically to dramatists, his insight bears repeating, for the tragic vision does not confine itself to drama. No "pinched and starved view of human nature" appears in any of Alice Brown's stories; instead, she rises above "sordid misery" to achieve a "truly tragic vision." This vision stands forth clearly in *Kings End* (1901) and in *Old Crow* (1922), both novels that deliberately probe the nature of, the uses of, suffering; and both comment significantly about the relationship between good and evil.

Convinced that man's own humanity sidetracks him in his goal of reaching happiness on earth, Alice Brown, in *Kings End*, presents happiness gone awry primarily because of man's emphasis on his material rather than on his spiritual being. She insists, however, that the material part aids in the formulation of the ideals through which it becomes relatively minor in importance. Thus, although the heroines in *Kings End* act under the stimulus of a highly idealized love-consisting-of-service attitude, the emphasis in the novel shifts from an examination of this attitude to a deeper and wider exploration of the Mary and Martha theme—the relationship between the spirit and the flesh, which, balanced and parallel, inhabit the same world in a necessary dependence.

Elder Kent of *Kings End*, an itinerant preacher who is accompanied by his sister Julie, inspires young, naïve, starry-eyed Nancy Eliot to vow a life of self-sacrifice, forsaking all others, after she hears the Elder preach at a Gospel meeting. For Nancy, such sacrifice would entail leaving home, family, and Martin Jeffers, the young man who wishes to marry her. Caught in this fantasy of self-sacrifice, but before she makes it actual, Nancy enmeshes herself in the problem of Luke Evans, atheist and free thinker. Luke attempts to care for his illegitimate baby daughter. He has stolen the baby from its loving grandparents who gave it a home after the death of their daughter, the baby's mother. Nancy, fired by her misguided ideals, considers immolation on the marriage altar as a better way of serving God than running off to preach. However, Julie Kent, whose life has been the continuous sacrifice of looking after the necessities of life for her preacher brother as they tramp the countryside together, prevents Nancy from making either sacrifice.

Nancy's stubborn and heartfelt plea that she wants to serve God forces Julie's rejoinder that she should then "be a good girl, and marry a man that wants you, and take care of him. Serve God! You don't have to tear yourself all to pieces to do it."[27] Julie admonishes Nancy out of her own experience as a woman whose deathbed promise to a demanding mother has caused her to relinquish her own right to happiness with a good man. As she tells Nancy, "You get to be an old woman and this is what you've learned. We're made to live here, here in this world. Time enough for another when you get there."[28]

Yet Julie's unwilling sacrifice reaps its own reward, for Elder Kent, after countless years of frightening his listeners in exhorting them to turn from their evil ways, finally reaches a higher vision in his preaching, healing, helping, and saving. In the tremendous five-town prayer meeting when his helper is moving everyone to sobs and anxiety, he himself stands by the platform with arms folded and face lifted peacefully to heaven. Love has replaced fear, and this love encompasses everyone: "Love of father and mother, wife and child, what are they but the love of God? Give yourself up to Him. Say every time you breathe, 'Lord, tell me what to do.' "[29]

As a higher instrument of God, Elder Kent saves Luke from despair; Luke, who curses his lot and whose "torturous way led back to the mysterious wrong of having himself been born,"[30] makes a "bargain" with God—the life of his sick baby daughter for the burning of his heretical books. But Elder Kent succeeds in assuring Luke that God is good and the world is good and "wrong is only goodness we don't understand."[31] In this conception of evil, the idea of original sin preached in an orthodox Christian view relegates itself to the discard; for the Elder tells Luke that "evil is one of the ways of God. If the bad man is bad, it is because he is ignorant of the road. He is taking a long, long path, when it might be shortened. But all roads lead home."[32] Such preaching is far removed from the hell-and-damnation variety, but it stands close to the vision of Greek tragedy. When Luke finally prays to God, "You made me. . . . You've got to see me through. I'll do what I can, but it's your business,"[33] Luke's conversion both to a saner view of reality and to a more contented life result.

As well as fostering the life that led her brother to his own maturity, Julie, directly through her own love-starved life, convinces Nancy that she must not give up her youth and beauty to follow a path that is alluring only because she contemplates it with youthful idealism. Having suffered the deprivation of love herself, she knows what such a life would hold for Nancy; she speaks with the authority of experience. A third reward comes to Julie when she learns that her renounced lover has remembered her in his will; for she feels supreme happiness for herself after his death, knowing now that he has held his love for her throughout a lifetime; and delighting in the happiness of Nancy and Martin, she realizes that "Nancy was no richer than she; only it was a different season of the year."[34]

Good and evil, as exemplified in *Kings End*, meet on the plain of suffering. So-called "sin" is in reality misunderstanding caused by lack of faith. This misunderstanding becomes faith through the kindness of others, through love which suffers without thought of recompense, although recompense always comes in unexpected ways as the curer himself is cured. Luke grows into faith through the despair born of the dark night of the soul; for on his way to commit suicide in a world indifferent to him, he hears Elder Kent calling him from a bog, which has sucked the preacher under to his armpits. The life-giving act, as well as the companionship that follows, gives Luke the impetus to take his step into faith; and as he follows the Elder who now preaches the love of God instead of the justice of God, Luke's life, for the first time, takes on a purpose.

Writing to the Reverend Joseph Mary Lelen on May 4, 1931, Alice Brown says, "I enclose a clipping to show my self-restraint. You know it is by W.R. Benét, husband of Elinor Wylie, and I want to write him, 'please, *please* do avoid grief. I can't have you suffer.' But one mustn't. For that's where God's great gift of human love comes in."[35] Suffering, for Alice Brown, as imaged in the lives of *Kings End*, leads to growth. In her view, evil, "only good we do not understand," helps toward the recognition that all mankind stands together in a brotherhood of pain, as previously noted. But this pain is necessary and good, for it not only helps one person to empathize with another, but it also aids him to revise his values. Both activities lead to a more mature view of reality. Thus, as shown previously in *A Day of His Youth* and *Margaret Warrener,* the high and the lowly recognize their brotherhood—a vital recognition—through pain.[36]

The story of *Kings End* flows simply with asides for the lighter story of Martin Jeffers as he, in despair, courts Nancy. The ideas, although insisted upon with sincerity, hover on the surface. The most interesting and important part of the novel—that concerning Luke's conversion from atheism and despair to faith and hope—appears through plot rather than through character development; for Luke remains a type, and is never a living character. An early novel (1901), *Kings End* interests primarily through the themes which, explored later with greater art, show the workings of Miss Brown's mind toward her own philosophy of life—a philosophy that more artfully, more carefully, and more complexly appears in *Old Crow*. As if the simplicity of the answers became apparent to Miss Brown as she realized the difficulties of applying these answers to more complex questions, a different perspective from which to view suffering and evil emerges in *Old Crow* (1922). It is difficult to resist the conclusion that, like her characters, Miss Brown herself matured through the suffering of the intervening years.

John Raven, protagonist of *Old Crow* and a middle-aged society dropout, hates "the whole blamed show." Sick of the "system, from the beasts that devour one another to the rest," he determines to desert, to run away, to do some thinking at Wake Hill, a family home that is as far out of the world as he can manage. Disgusted with the lack of moral fiber displayed by society after World War I, Raven feels that the world has gone crazy; and he tells his young friend Nan that he is going to give up his business because he hates it and he hates "the whole business of what we call civilized life."[37]

Raven's dissatisfaction stems also from his own life. Brought up by a father who thought he "was God," Raven suffered later in life because of a woman much older than he who demanded and received a nooselike devotion from him. This woman, Nan's Aunt Anne, would not allow Nan to show childish affection to him, but she could not kill the deep love that grew between him and Nan.

As the story opens, Raven, preparatory to seeking his hideaway, writes his nephew Dick, who is desperately trying to win Nan's promise to marry him, to explain how the world appears to him and to comment about his dropping out of an existence that he can no longer support. Raven, who speaks almost in despair, tells Dick that "we are not made in the image of God. We are made rather grotesquely out of dust."

To Raven, all the plans men make for defeating death and time also return men to dust. Even though God made men, they can never discover His will, can never hope for "an alleviation of misery on our dark planet." All the inventions men make to alleviate disease and poverty "shall unloose as many by-products of discovery and bring new plagues upon us."[38] So, as Raven turns from God, he feels himself uncared for, and without a reason for sustaining his existence. Having once experienced God in his hopes for mankind, Raven has now lost Him, together with all his hopes and dreams. Although he has seriously considered suicide, he has rejected this solution, fearing that it would not result in his complete destruction but perhaps cause him to appear again on earth in another form. Now, finding civilization sickening, he intends to seek in Wake Hill the physical labor that will enable him at least to sleep nights.

Dick, a right-thinking, conventional young man, is appalled by his uncle's decision to drop out of society; and he convinces himself that Raven needs a psychiatrist. But Raven speaks out in language that has become commonplace fifty years later: "How do you know it isn't the healthiest thing that ever happened in this rotten tissue of pretense we call civilization for even one man—just one—to get up and swear at the whole system and swear again that, so far as his little midge's existence goes, he won't subscribe to it? What business have you to call that disease? How do you know it isn't health? How do you know I'm not one of the few normal atoms in the whole blamed carcass?"[39]

Yet even at Wake Hill, Raven's dreams fill with frightening shadows as he envisions the troubles of an "unceasing panorama, a pageant of pain and death" in which "every atom of creation was against every other atom" because "everywhere was warfare, murder and rapine, for the mere chance of living."[40] He feels himself part of this horror while listening to the animals who are engaged in the war to the death; and Raven hates the fact that God had made it so and that God did not care. Giving vent to his dissatisfaction with the way things are and seeking a purpose for his life, Raven resembles today's lamenting-over-life hero, but with a difference: Raven finds an answer.

For into the quiet where the days are peaceful, even if the nights are not, comes beautiful young Tira, a country girl married to an insanely jealous husband, and Tira's baby, who the husband believes in his jealousy has been fathered by another. Tira, who has been rescued from an evil life by her husband Tenny, pays for the rescue with loyalty beyond any reasonable expectation. She refuses to leave Tenny, even though he forces her time and time again to take the baby and flee his insane wrath and threats against the baby. Meeting Tira on one occasion when she flees from Tenny, Raven arranges that any time Tenny threatened to have one of his insane fits, she go for refuge to a little cottage in the woods (a cottage in which Raven's grand-uncle Old Crow lived for many years before his death and in which he wrote a journal that he left to Raven).

The story weaves back and forth between Tira's tragedy and Raven's dawning faith. Raven finds out through the journal that Old Crow had once felt exactly as he himself now feels; he too had lost his faith and had ranted against the cruelty and injustice of a rapacious and sick world. But Old Crow, through befriending an old, poor, sick degenerate, Billy Jones, had regenerated himself by taking Billy Jones to the cottage and caring for him until the old man's death, despite the epithet "crazy" afforded this service by the town people. Old Crow even lied about his lack of faith to comfort the dying Billy Jones who had once killed a man and who wished to be assured he had been forgiven. Old Crow gave this assurance to comfort Billy Jones; and through a vision at Billy Jones' death, Old Crow received the gift of faith.

Like Old Crow, Raven regenerates himself, but he does so through his love of Tira. Like Old Crow before him, Raven lies for Tira; he gives her a comfort he himself lacks by assuring her that she lives in the presence of Christ, thereby enabling her to live without fear, even though she must guard herself and her baby against her husband. When tragedy finally overtakes Tira—Tenny in jealous rage smothers the baby—Tira drowns herself in grief at her loss and in an attempt to extricate Raven from her troubles. Raven, even though his love for Tira has been the sustaining power of his life, understands Tenny's behavior; he feels that Tenny had found the difficulties of life too much for him and had revolted. He assures Tenny (as Old Crow had assured Billy Jones before him, and with just as much lack of conviction) that he has been forgiven. Fortunately, Raven is saved from Tenny's devotion and care (as Old Crow had not been saved from Billy Jones') by Tenny's being put into a sanitarium where psychiatry might have a try at piecing together a life that had "tried to right the balance of some of the most mysteriously devilish inequalities a poorly equipped chap ever found himself up against."[41]

Raven finally acknowledges his love for Nan. Even though the faith he attempts to touch lacks substance, it promises to build on love instead of despair; and Raven will fight the battle of life instead of deserting. Old Crow, the instrument that prods Raven to a new awareness, has discovered order in man's universe—an order existentially following inexorable law, just as, in ecstasy a moment after Billy Jones' death, he experiences existence itself. Old Crow passes this discovery on to Raven in his journal:

I saw that creation had been a long time going on. I saw that although we have minds to think with, we haven't really, in comparison with the things to be thought out. I saw that we are so near the dust that we can no more account for the ways of Almighty God than the owl hooting out there in the woods can read the words I am writing here. I saw that nothing is to be told us. We are to find out everything for ourselves, just as we have found electricity and the laws of physics. And poisons—we have found out those, some of them, even if we had to die to do it. And God lets us die trying to find out. He doesn't care anything about our dying. He doesn't care anything about the rabbit broken by the owl, or the toad struck by the snake.[42]

Yet the legacy passed on to Raven is not pessimistic; hope covers fear, for Old Crow finds the reason for suffering symbolized in the life of Christ, whose death is the "everlasting symbol of man's duty; to die for another."[43] He finds that the horrible sacrifices of man's past and present—and future—lead to the real sacrifice, man's own heart. Raven, finding that his life and Old Crow's had run parallel courses, accepts the message of hope. Both had been victims of world sickness; both had been healed.

Just as Old Crow frees Raven from the tyranny of his own hopeless outlook, so Tira frees him from the tyranny of Anne. Raven comes to full maturity as he realizes that most of his life has been spent under the authority of others—first his father's, then Anne's—because he had been simply too resigned to protest, to fight. But Old Crow has shown him that the fight is all, even while the goal remains nebulous; that just as early man could not conceive of electricity, so present-day man cannot conceive of future wonders. Suffering—as exemplified for Raven by his despair over society's lack of ideals, as well as his unrequited love for Tira and by his resignation to the wills of his father and Anne—has enabled him to grow. Just as Raven has had to blunder along in his attempts to find solutions, so mankind must blunder along in its attempts to make a brighter and more mature society. However, the struggle, both individually and collectively, need not be made in darkness; for the symbols of Christ's life light the way to love in the brotherhood of pain which leads to the goal of growth and maturity. Thus Raven joins Margaret Warrener and other protagonists of Miss Brown in learning the value of suffering.

An interesting sidelight on the generation gap appears when Raven considers his nephew Dick who had been "brought up against life as it looks when you see it naked, the world—and what a world! No wonder he swore it was a world such as neither he nor his fellows, like him aghast, would have made. He would simply have to live some quarter century to find out what sort of a world he and his fellows did actually make." The key to the good life, to the mystery of life, will not be found by youth: "And yet, and yet, hasn't all youth held the key for that borrowed interval and do the walls ever really fall?"[44]

To what key does Miss Brown refer? Is it the innocence of ideals not yet tarnished; the goodness of intention not yet miscarried; the certainty of faith not yet shaken? Whatever it is, she insists that age must include youth in its understanding, as youth, except for the poets, cannot possibly include age. And the paradox of a paradise lost in a fortunate fall disappears in contemplation of the fact that—even though for both old and young living is terrifying, cruel, seemingly unjust—growth in understanding and sympathy gained through living and through using evil to evolve good sustain the courageous. Life must be lived; only the cowardly drop out of it.

In *Old Crow* good and evil, love and suffering, are not only inexplicably related; they are interdependent. Christian symbols point to the greater reality, showing man that, although all humanity blunders into evil, good rises from the pain as maturity and growth come from the understanding that "evil is only good we do not understand." As evil works through good, the pain suffered leads to new growth. The groping toward this clear conviction in *Old Crow* results in some confusion of ideas; in fact, one tends to forget, through the involvement with the philosophical and theological premises under which Miss Brown operates, that this is a novel. As Raven cannot satisfactorily, with certainty, resolve all of his doubts, Miss Brown reveals herself to be in the same predicament. Unlike *Kings End,* in which both Elder Kent and Luke Evans reach a certainty, *Old Crow* reveals a more mature and more thoughtful reaction to existence. Alice Brown apparently has learned that maturity carries with it the onus of confessing that one does not have all the answers.

The prescribed time of life for Alice Brown's characters (like John Phillips Marquand's and Saul Bellow's) to attempt new questions is the mid-forties—the age in which youth culminates in a supposedly mature outlook, albeit a time of introspection and retrospection. Alice Brown's characters, unlike the modern novelist's, do not resign themselves to frustration. Raven works out his problem through service to others; and in this service, as well as in wisdom learned from an older and wiser Old Crow, he gains a more hopeful philosophy. As man is responsible for man, the old and the wise must help the young and the immature; for both, the help depends upon the working through of evil to good by suffering.

This interrelation of aspects of good and evil (considered from a moral point of view) or of constructive and destructive behavior (considered from a psychological point of view) apparently receives support from no less an authority than Dr. Albert Ellis, although he would not support the moral terminology. Dr. Ellis points out:

There exists a kind of balanced ecological relationship between the appearance of certain human traits and other (desirable and undesirable) traits; and if one outstanding trait were somehow eliminated or pronouncedly emphasized, the effects that would ensue are almost impossible to imagine. . . . There may be various other disadvantages, moreover, to changing the basic biological structure of human beings, even if this becomes (as it is increasingly becoming) quite possible to do. If the biological basis of neurosis were completely overcome, it is possible that men and women would be too alike and undifferentiated to enjoy each other very much; that they would eventually lose much of their motivation for living and striving (including the challenge of working with and trying to surmount their own biological limitations).[45]

Raven illustrates the attempt to surmount his own biological limitations against both Dick's and his sister Amelia's insistence that he should consult a psychiatrist when, almost in despair, he drops out of a society that he considers cruel and ruthless. But Raven surmounts his problems through involvement with Tira and her troubles and, more importantly, through the insight that Old Crow passes on to him—an insight founded on Alice Brown's often-reiterated belief that there may be indeed more to existence than the bit of life here on this earth that man can at present experience, together with the conviction that suffering (neurosis?) does give "motivation for living and striving." Although Alice Brown would not deny the benefits of psychiatry to those beyond normal friendly help (she commits Tenny to the sanitarium for such specialized help), the importance of self-help—coupled with the aid of others, such as friends, relatives, acquaintances—becomes the basis for the solution to the problem of living. This was previously pointed out in the short stories. Alice Brown appears to be saying in *Old Crow* that the lack of imagination to see the tremendous advantage of self-growth through suffering may keep the psychiatrist's couch constantly occupied; and lack of courage to work through a problem and to gain all the ensuing advantage of doing so causes the failure of an individual both to reach his own potential and to assist his brother to reach his. For Alice Brown, loving means suffering, and suffering means growth; it is doubtful that anyone who has truly loved would not agree.

It is not surprising that *The New York Times* called *Old Crow* one of the finest of Alice Brown's novels and that Hugh Walpole selected it as one of the six best American novels of 1922.[46] Aspects of human behavior presented make it psychologically and sociologically sound, even in the light of today's knowledge. More important, its current relevance rests firmly on a view of human nature that, as Ellis suggests, is vital and necessary for human development and happiness.

CHAPTER 5

Morality versus Convention

"T HE Poet's Vision and the Power Divine" is Lilian Whiting's tribute that acknowledges the height from which Alice Brown views existence. The Victorian idealism of Miss Brown manifests itself clearly in her choice of unconventional heroines and heroes, who endure the buffetings of man-made conventions without any real rebellion against them. The suffering caused by flaunting of convention, either through intention or through the betrayal by others, leads these protagonists not to change convention but rather to accept in humility what exists in society. In addition to unconventional morality, Alice Brown explores the restraints upon individuality imposed by conventional mores, particularly as seen through the conflict between desire and duty as it pertains to husbands. Miss Brown apparently finds that, paradoxical as it appears to be, individual growth can be obtained through the renunciation of self-seeking accomplishments and the embracing of modes of behavior proper to one's status in life.

I *Women Betrayed*

The problem of women without wedding bands, victims of man's inhumanity in a man-made world, is scrutinized in the stories of two unconventional heroines who stand against the world in the novels *Rose MacLeod* (1908) and *The Story of Thyrza* (1909). Like Miss Brown's male protagonists, both refuse to be crushed by the world and its rules; instead, they fight convention as well as injustice; and in the battle, they realize their own potentialities. Rose MacLeod, a worldly, sophisticated Parisienne, and Thyrza, a naive, unsophisti-

cated country girl, suffer disillusionment and heartbreak
because of misplaced love; but both overcome the destruction of their illusions to reach a happiness that far surpasses
the illusory one.

The characters in *Rose MacLeod* are built on contrasts.
Rose MacLeod, common-law wife of Electra Fulton's dead
brother, Tom, seeks escape from the influence of her father
in Tom's family; for Markham MacLeod, an extremely pow-
erful labor leader, had "sold" her to Tom and is now about
to "sell" her to a member of royalty. Rose's cold reception
by Electra Fulton, however, drives her to the home of her
friend, Peter Grant, a young man with whom she has come
from Paris to New England and who, living alongside of the
Fultons, expects to marry Electra. The story's plot is slight,
and it ends with Rose's forthcoming marriage to Osmond,
Peter's brother.

Electra, in direct contrast to Rose, is "distinctly American
and typical of her day, well-born, well-educated, capable
and consciously well-bred."[1] Her consciousness of her
place in society and of her breeding lead Electra to become
the hypocritical supporter of ideals that she fails to maintain.
Taking life to be of high seriousness, she steps blindly upon
Markham MacLeod's bandwagon, eager to work for his
"Brotherhood"; but she fails to extend a hand to Rose Mac-
Leod, who desperately needs a friend; indeed, she scorns
Rose because she does not wear a wedding ring. Although
Rose MacLeod fails to receive hospitality at Electra's, Peter
Grant's family, consisting of his brother, Osmond, and
Granny, receive her with delight and love. Contrast appears
again between Peter and Osmond: Peter, a young artist,
extremely talented and successful, has been financed in his
study and in his European living through the labor of Osmond, labor literally done in tilling the soil. Peter, handsome, with a great artistic gift, is a naïve idealist, even
though he has lived in the world and traveled in worldly
circles. Osmond, a deformed, earthy laborer who never
leaves his "plantation," is a simple, good, honest man whose
imagination extends far beyond that of his brother's, even
though this imagination consists of making a new world for
Rose and himself as they meet in the open at night with a

touch of "fantastic romanticism that is faintly reminiscent of
Peter Ibbetson."[2]

Idealistic to the highest degree, Osmond regards love as
the greatest mortal attainment "not so much the possession
of it, but the guarding of it for all the uses of the world."[3]
Although Osmond must live in the open, apparently because
of some lung trouble that has made him a hunchback (although this is not explicit), he does win the love of Rose;
and primarily through her persistent wooing, he resolves to
take his chances in a society not willing to receive him as a
normal human being, even though his life up to that time
had ill fitted him for the intricacies of a citified existence.

Contrast again appears in the characterization of Madam
Fulton, Electra's grandmother, and Bessie Grant, Peter's
grandmother. Florrie Fulton, a spoiled but lovable old lady
who had attempted to live a life of excitement, gave up
Charlie Grant in favor of marrying Mark Fulton, a Cambridge
professor who promised to give her a better life than the
country doctor, Charlie Grant, could. But Florrie now discovers in her aged clarity that Bessie has had the excitement
as well as the joy and the peace in life instead of her, even
though Bessie's life has been one of service, particularly to
Osmond whom she literally saved from death by living with
him in the open for months at a time and by fostering the
strength from the rugged outdoor existence that enabled
him to overcome his physical weakness. Unlike Florrie,
who lived for herself, constantly attempting to outdistance
the boredom such self-centered existence brought her,
Bessie lived for Osmond, continuously praying in certitude
of God's love as sustaining shield against life's hardships.
Serenely, she tells Peter never to doubt the kindness of God
when Peter fears that Osmond's deformity will prevent
his marriage to Rose.

The contrasts in characterization emphasize paradoxes
that reveal truth as Miss Brown sees it: Rose, cynical and
worldly, has become warm and good, undoubtedly through
the honesty in outlook that cynicism has fostered; Electra,
sheltered, well-bred, has become hard and hypocritical,
apparently from lack of experience in the world, which
caused her to remain no more than a child. Again, Florrie

Fulton, gay and charming, eager for all life has to offer, ends in disillusionment and in the certainty that Bessie's life has been better than hers for, forced by her frustrations to live an illusory life in memoirs that she fabricates, she knows her own life to be bland and uninteresting. On the other hand, Bessie, secure in her faith, knows the contentment of having helped in creating Osmond, and she enjoys the peace of a life spent in service. But Peter and Osmond strike the heart of the paradox: Peter, the artist, despite his great gift for form and color, remains the naïve idealist, shallow and happy, skimming the surface of life while drunk on its beauty; Osmond, the earthy laborer, becomes the strong doer, passionate and determined, experiencing life because he has had to wrest it from overpowering forces of disease and convention.

Mary Ford, in an early review of *Rose MacLeod*, complains that the love interest between Rose and Osmond is somewhat unreal and unsatisfactory—a little too transcendental to rank as lovemaking outside of New England. Miss Ford also feels that Osmond's deformity should be made clearer, as one does not know exactly what the two lovers had to overcome to approach a normal life with each other.[4] Miss Ford praises the characterization of Electra, which she compares to Imogen Upton in Anne Douglas Sedgwick's *A Fountain Sealed;* she states that Miss Brown and Miss Sedgwick "have contributed another distinct personality to the Portrait Gallery of American women."[5] Miss Ford's judgment of unreality and dissatisfaction concerning the love affair might be acceptable if one denies the major premise upon which the argument for this love builds. For Miss Brown, the transcendental nature of love raises the sights from the real and the satisfactory to the imaginative and the illusive. No explicit scenes of love in its physical passion appear, but Miss Brown de-emphasizes clearly the physical in order to emphasize that the souls of Rose and Osmond meet in love; they have almost instantaneously accomplished the goal that a lifetime of physical passion and groping communication ordinarily requires—the complete blending of two human personalities in love.

Although Electra might be considered to be a "distinct

personality," the lack of depth in her presentation makes her rather a type; and little imagination need be used to understand her intensity of sham emotion, which covers her inability to submit to honesty in emotion and in life. Rose and Osmond, however, speak to a heightened awareness, a sharpened imagination, which is willing to allow that perhaps other eyes see other things, that perhaps experiences exist which science cannot explain nor technology produce. Rose and Osmond speak to faith and hope.

Rose has not allowed worldly wisdom to cloud her innate goodness. Victim of a colossal evil perpetrated by her free-thinking father who used her to further his own power by "selling" her to a prince for a mistress, Rose remains innocent of evil herself, even as she cynically views a hostile world. Her saving grace resides in the love (or what passed for it) offered her by a charming, though rascally, father throughout a happy childhood. When she realizes to her sorrow that this love became subservient to his desire for power, the strength of her own personality (a strength fostered by suffering duty to villainous Tom Fulton, who also exploited her goodness) enables her to remain free from sordid taint in her own estimation. This lack of guilt allows her to love freely when Osmond's love presents itself. A father's inhumanity to an adoring daughter and a man's inhumanity to a loving common-law wife have not succeeded in killing faith and hope; Rose MacLeod rises above her tormentors to live maturely and fully in love.

Like Rose MacLeod, another heroine who speaks to faith and hope is presented in *The Story of Thyrza*, although almost an entire lifetime ensues before Thyrza bows in acknowledgment to them. Instead, courage informs her life— courage born from an exaggerated sense of commitment to sacrificing her life for others. Like Nancy in *Kings End*, Thyrza, highly imaginative, extremely sensitive, and supremely emotional, succeeds in overpowering with sheer force of personality a loving but weaker mother. But unlike Nancy, who has reached some maturity, Thyrza is only nine years old at the start of the novel, a heroine unique to Miss Brown, who ordinarily does not portray children. But motivation for plot depends upon Thyrza's character as revealed

in early life, and Miss Brown portrays excellently, apparently from memories of her own childhood, the great burden of
emotion striving for expression in nine-year-old Thyrza,
emotion that remains inarticulate throughout Thyrza's entire life.

The novel spans Thyrza's life from preadolescence;
through young womanhood, when misplaced passion leads
her to mistake it for love and to her having an illegitimate
child whom she refuses to lie about but in whom she attempts to instill her own uncompromising attitude about
truth and with life; to middle-age. Petrie, her son, becomes
well-educated entirely through his mother's at-home
sewing; but he lacks the maturity to recognize the nobility
of his mother's life until his fiancée contrives with Thyrza
to help him grow up.

A review in *The Atlantic Monthly* stated that this novel
was unconvincing because the presentation was so frag-
mentary, and the reviewer considered Thyrza to be an incon-
sistent sketch of a type often done, such as Jane Eyre. The
reviewer also faulted dramatic causality, stating that Thyrza,
as presented, would not have acted as she did merely through
force of circumstance; and Miss Brown was presumed not
to have enough knowledge of human passion to make the
story believable.[6] Another review of the novel in *The Independent* considered that the situation of the novel, mon-
strous as it is, was almost entirely another product of tragic
New England fiction and lacked credibility—particularly
in its closing when Thyrza goes to live in the home left her
by a fine man who has loved her from her girlhood days and
when she ends philosophizing on sin with her sister.[7]

While some of this criticism might be justified, there are
also depths not hinted at in the reviews. Thyrza, like many
children, suffers much cruelty at the hands of both Rosie
May—her pretty playmate who has all the beauty Thyrza
lacks, who knows it, and who is the "last living creature
before whom Thyrza can be her simple self"[8]—and the un-
thinking adult who refers to Thyrza in her presence as a
"picked chicken." For Thyrza, one of the good people designed by fate to be hurt by the insensitive, has a superego
that compels her to lead what she calls a "consecrated life"

as she hurries to do tasks so that others might not have to do them. She is enormously conscious all the time of this consecration which leads her to a "longing to give people what they never desired for themselves."[9] Living only an inward life and feeding on unrealistic dreams, she is forever "painting the picture in dazzling colors, and the world . . . as regularly toning it down."[10]

The portrayal of Thyrza at nine clearly reveals the overpowering compensation of a homely, thin, poor waif who must feed her inward starvation with an uncontrolled imagination in which largesse and goodness result in a "passionate giving like the fruit that drops, in a large radius, from a spreading tree";[11] for Thyrza is a "glutton for praise" and a "word of reproof reduced her to penury." This completely believable and enchanting child, lively and intelligent above the norm, succeeds on two counts: she bests Rosie May by destroying her playhouse (a cruel and unheard-of action), and she gains the attention of wealthy, well-educated Barton Gosse, who tutors her. Both incidents teach her the source of power: offense (in the case of Rosie May) and intellect (as she parses Latin verbs and reads Virgil for Barton Gosse). However, both sources fail to attain sufficient force: her scrupulosity compels her to set the playhouse straight (but only after Rosie May has seen it destroyed), and her consecration to goodness prevents her later marrying Barton Gosse lest he be tainted by being thought her son's father. Yet she has learned; for later, when Barton's sister Helen suffers a broken heart and social disgrace because of having run off with a married man, Thyrza feels that Helen, having taken a "forbidden way . . . should have been colossal in it, a beacon, not a frail figure."[12]

Thyrza, then, is presented not simply but in all the complexities of striving with and against both innate characteristics and early influences; and she falls for the passionate, if temporary, need of Andy whom she believes loves her and wishes to marry her, although in reality Andy loves and marries her sister Laura. Only Thyrza's habit of dreaming, rather than seeing, truth stands as motivation for her downfall. Faced with the impossibility of ruining her sister's

happiness (for Andy married Laura immediately after
Thyrza wrote him about her pregnancy), Thyrza comes to a
plausible solution: a life away from home and family will be
her sacrifice for the son whom she feels she has cheated out
of the inheritance of a good name. Thyrza's dedicated life-
habits serve in sustaining her in hardship, for she raises
the hardships to the level of sacrifice for Petrie, her son.
Truth becomes her weapon, for "all her undying hope had
been in drawing straight lines."[13] But she remains unaware
that Petrie, when a small boy, has had to fight the boys who
taunted him about his illegitimacy; the truth about his birth,
which Thyrza armed him with, did not win the battle. Petrie
is the Realist; Thyrza, the Romanticist. Thyrza "must keep
the bonds of punishment she had meted out to herself"[14]

Barton Gosse sees the hardships of Thyrza's life to be of
her own making as he tells her that she shut herself up in a
prison, determined to serve out her sentence—not that she
tried to be too good, but that she didn't "believe enough
. . . in the thing that makes over and renews."[15] Thyrza
has made people into the avenging Furies she had read
about as a child with Barton—the first was Rosie May, made
into a torturer by Thyrza and vanquished and turned into a
little girl again by Thyrza's courage in battling her by means
of the destruction of the playhouse. The second, perhaps,
was Andy; and she can finally turn him into a not very
admirable person but yet a mere man deserving of forgive-
ness; Laura, the "last Fury left . . . dwindled into
something human like herself."[16]

Thus Thyrza's uncontrolled, imaginary life has made her
real life one of hardship and suffering. And yet—Alice
Brown intimates—the conclusion hovers mysteriously; for
Thyrza, able at last to turn Petrie over to his fiancée, able,
if she wishes, to marry Barton Gosse for a life of joy, must
face one last trial. Barton Gosse, injured in an automobile
accident, dies in her arms; but he has left her a legacy both
of material wealth and of hope for an afterlife of fulfillment—desires symbolized by the imprisoned music in the
piano she had always longed for, for her desires were always
beyond "the surge of life."[17] But the trial is won, for she now
has learned that she can transcend the mistakes of the past;

and if she wishes, she can travel to gain the intellectual and artistic stature of a Barton Gosse. She knows, however, that the harmony of the day she meets him again will not depend on an intellectual or artistic equality but will spring simply from "the old, old love of righteousness."[18]

And although Thyrza has experienced disillusionment throughout life from the evil of another, as well as from her own failure to assess reality properly; has failed to fulfill her promise; and has stagnated through a misplaced sense of duty, she finds at the end of the novel her reason for living (and it is Alice Brown's reason also)—to bring hope, the greatest gift of all.

II *Desire and Duty*

Victorian idealism shows itself no more strongly than in the acceptance of duty over the desire to shirk duty for self-fulfillment. The two most interesting novels that clearly emphasize the importance of, and the rewards of, duty are *John Winterbourne's Family* (1910) and *Dear Old Templeton* (1927). Each novel has as protagonist a middle-aged man who is forced by commitment, rather than by wish, to care for a wife to whom he is no longer bound by love. The value of adhering to solemn promises, not only to the recipient but also to the giver of the promises, forms the basis of each novel.

John Winterbourne's Family, which is characterized by "quiet sentiment and gentle humor in which Alice Brown gives her fancy free play by affectionately showing a whimsical character in a combination of homely New England experience and Greek myth,"[19] presents John Winterbourne at a turning point in his life, a point at which he must choose service to self or service to others in an Existential choice that will determine his final being. When the novel opens, John Winterbourne, perfectly content with a bachelor's existence, confides to his friend, young Jim Lovell, that his life suits him perfectly, that he could live forever with his housekeeper, Lyddy, to fix his meals. He wants to smoke his pipe, take his daily swim, enjoy his book and his fire—and wishes for nothing more. But into his rural paradise unexpectedly comes his family consisting of his wife (who is returning to

him from an amicable separation because she has spent all
the money he had settled on her), his adopted daughter
Celia, and Celia's recently found sister Bess.

John Winterbourne, like John Raven in *Old Crow*, has
dropped out of society but through inertia rather than disgust; and he revels in his leisurely contemplation of his
Greek-New England world, aided and abetted by two young
friends, Jim Lovell and Dwight Hunter. Jim and Dwight,
each for his own considered reason, have also dropped out
of society. All three, however, find a woman the force that
compels them toward living all of life as it is, rather than
allowing them to merely regard the passing of its panorama.
John Winterbourne accepts the care of his wife, and Jim
Hunter and Dwight Lovell make themselves hostages of
fortune by falling in love and planning a life with one of
John's daughters.

Unlike John Raven, however, John Winterbourne had
made peace with his existence (or believed he had) by taking
refuge in a rural paradise that he inhabited in imagination
with Greek gods. But the peace is shattered by the one who
had sent him toward it in the first place—Catherine his wife,
who loves him passionately. Catherine attempts to live life
by assuming responsibilities for bettering the world, and
her very intensity "made him resolve in a reactionary spite
that he would have none."[20] Catherine and Winterbourne
represent the two extremes of action and contemplation;
and like Robert Frost's "Stopping by Woods on a Snowy
Evening," *John Winterbourne's Family* presents one man's
response to the dilemma without attempting to resolve the
dilemma itself.

Yet John Winterbourne matures as a human being when
he is literally forced to live up to the "biggest of promissory
notes" he had given his wife when he married her. He realizes that "the idea of choosing a way of life required fidelity
to the choice";[21] and even though he has felt himself completely content in his wayward existence, he comes to recognize that, when he swears to Jupiter, it is because he
"dared not" challenge the God of all because, if he did,
"he might hear answers."[22] The Pagan has been replaced
by the Christian.

Dropping out of a life equates itself with failure to adhere to the duty inherent in the choice one has freely made, just as complete reliance on the gods equates itself with failure to act freely as a human being. Winterbourne realizes this fact when Mrs. Ramsay, a neighbor and a compulsive do-gooder (whom he calls Mrs. Jellyby for obvious reasons), breaks down physically and relies on the strength of his household, just as the five Ramsay children have been re-lying on his personal strength as their informal counselor. In musing about Mrs. Ramsay's life—that of lecturing, pro-testing, fighting for causes, a life lived to the detriment of her own household of husband and children—Winterbourne sees that Mrs. Ramsay must, sick or well, "go home to her own job." Having seen Mrs. Ramsay's duty, he also realizes that the "cap he had meant for Mrs. Ramsay had been sud-denly caught by some breeze of fancy, whirled about and settled on his own head, and to his pathetic terror, it fitted."[23] And as he asks himself what if the house, the wife, and the attendant train of circumstances were his job, just as Mrs. Ramsay's gold-topped children were hers, he begins to realize that choosing to contemplate existence from afar is different from choosing to set one's foot on one particular path; the chosen path must be followed to its end.

As Winterbourne resolves to stay with his wife, becoming kind to her because of her need of him during the nervous breakdown she suffers through strain of her unrequited love for him, he recognizes that the intellect he has been cultivat-ing as the highest good, the things graven on his brain, will vanish into dust; but what lives is "what's been kind. It's what has helped some other heart to live."[24] The selfishness of Winterbourne's existence, like that of John Raven's in *Old Crow*, has been transformed into a self-sacrificing responsi-bility; and he realizes that, in leaving the comforts of his self-centered but seemingly satisfying life, he has left the stagnation of sterile existence and climbed to a higher level. His life now counts because he lives in the kindness done for another.

Catherine grows, also, through suffering thwarted ambi-tion on behalf of her two adopted daughters, Celia and Bess. In realizing that no one really loves her, Catherine's introspection causes her to wonder at Bess's power to draw love to herself and to wonder whether the secret might be that "Bess demanded nothing and fed other minds without disturbing them."[25] She gains the strength to accept the devotion of Winterbourne without demanding the'love he cannot give, or the ability she cannot attain to see for a time with his eyes. As Catherine matures in her ability to accept herself with all her insecurities, she lessens the stranglehold on husband, thereby enabling him, in turn, to respond to her needs.

Celia, spoiled, pampered, but lacking the one gift that Catherine could not provide, the only one that would have enabled Celia to be at peace with herself—acceptance of her personality in love—begins to grow also through the unstinting love of her sister Bess. She sees that Bess's distinction —the difference between her and her whining, complaining world—is that Bess does something all the time. She sets her hand to hard things for the comfort of others—evidently the way to "keep alive." Life (service to others) conquers death (service to oneself) in Winterbourne and also in his family.

Bess, the model for Winterbourne, Catherine, and Celia, had to make her own way as a tavern worker. Living in service to all and sundry who come within her range, she has the "masterly sense to see that she, too, must be saved."[26] Bess, no languishing martyr, believes in the imminence of God without speculating about it; and she also believes that each person must be allowed freedom to be himself without coercion. This quality she perceives and loves in Winterbourne, whom she considers one who is "just kind and allowed you to be free."[27] The homely wisdom and the kind service Bess affords all stem from the common sense that perceives the need and fulfills it without speculating on the cause. Winterbourne finds Bess's great charm to consist in this ability—a charm his wife lacks, since she must continuously sift, sort, and pile evidence for actions that might better be done merely because they are kind. Winterbourne comes to accept that "the greatest . . . is charity."

A review of *John Winterbourne's Family* in the *Literary Digest* regarded the book as interesting but as not convincing; it contained some good theories on making the best of bad bargains; it threw a strong light on the "inadequacy of that which is wholly artificial"; and it had some parts that would "repay thoughtful reading."[28] The main theme of the novel appears to go deeper, however, than merely investigating making the best of bad bargains. It concerns fundamental duty of husband and wife to family, the same duty recognized by Martin Redfield in *My Love and I* when he resolved not only to take care of his wife materially but also to do his best to make her happy. Furthermore, Winterbourne's commitment indicates that such commitment carries with it rewards not only to the one served but also to the server. Winterbourne, in order to live instead of stultify, must take up the burden he had once freely chosen; for the dropout who evades the responsibility of his free choice drops out of life itself. The self-fulfillment that John Winterbourne expected to obtain through his relinquishment of once-chosen ties comes only when he accepts these ties; only then does he begin to fulfill his potentialities. Parts of the book will, even today, "repay thoughtful reading."

In *Dear Old Templeton,* a middle-aged writer whose books have become old-fashioned in a sophisticated age, longs to sally forth like a knight on the quest for the real meaning of life. Like John Winterbourne, he is frustrated by his duty to care for his family in a mundane existence; and he must discover what meaning he can while he is a prisoner of family ties. As Templeton cares for his wife Amy, who has been severely injured in an accident, he becomes the shining knight to Elizabeth, a young schoolteacher with a tremendous thirst for knowledge who takes care of his house much in the way Bess ministers to Winterbourne. Like Bess, Elizabeth falls in love with her elderly knight; and although her love also remains unrequited, her secret adoration sustains her as she finds her happiness in service to the beloved and, through him, to all in need of it.

Amy Templeton, like Mrs. Ramsay in *John Winterbourne's Family,* has been so busy lecturing and pursuing pseudointellectual activities until the time of her accident that she had reduced her husband to the status of housekeeper, a role he genially, if not happily, accepted, until Elizabeth brought her willing hands and her adoring heart to his succor. Pat, Templeton's scoundrel brother, steals his idea for a great novel, vulgarizes it, and makes a great financial success of it, thus thwarting Templeton's one chance at greatness. Sally, Templeton's daughter—a young girl with "invisible playmates" and a sixth sense, filled with disillusionment and jaded with the generation of which she is part—seeks and finds solace and advice from her father.

Like Winterbourne, Templeton gains the insight to recognize that suffering may bring human growth and that only kindness never perishes. His wife suffers serious injuries that will cripple her for life when she is hit by a car driven by Irene, a modern maid bent on self-destruction because of frustrated love for Champney, a young man who refuses to succumb to her lure of sex. Champney, who is in love with Sally, finally persuades her to marry him; and Templeton, who contentedly gives himself to the service of his wife, finds in this way the answers he would not have found had he not been forced to give up his knightly quest.

Templeton comes close to being a perfect human being, according to Alice Brown's standards; for he does what has to be done and suffers silently the wounds from others. He takes no action when Pat plagiarizes his story, but he finds consolation in the knowledge that nothing lasts, that his frustration was only that of

. . . one human purpose, a selfish purpose too, the apologetic guise the instinct for continuance takes on; to leave something behind us when we have gone hence? The roadside weed is trampled before it flowers, the tree is cut down in its fulness of years. Nothing lasts. . . . What does last is the invisible, the love that is the incense of life, the smoke of sacrifice, and that only flies upward like the vapor of man's breath and, to man's eyes at least, disappears. Perhaps it reaches that unattainable erection of human imagination known as the throne of God—but to what end? To please God, to buy his favor? Such matters were too deep for him. He did not know. This was not ordered thought. It was only feeling, over in a moment and amounting to a recognition that he had to be busy now with other things than the commemorative table of his life's testimony.[29]

As Templeton has built his life on the acceptance of others, all come to him for advice, even Pat, who later betrays his trust. Templeton, who sees that existence is surrounded by mystery, feels that it is "as impenetrable as if we hadn't made an electric light bulb and couldn't talk about complexes."[30] He attempts to place Pat in proper perspective to his place in the universe: "When we began to learn so much about the wonders of the universe, it shouldn't have taken us farther away from beauty and tranquility and all the things that make life worth while. When we invented motors, we should have looked on them as something to translate life into wonder, not stinking djinns that enable us to 'go some place' without seeing what we pass on the way. And I'd have everything that's invented referred to the highest intelligence we've got to show us how to use it, and not turned over to demos, to make louder smash-bangs and nastier smells."[31] But Pat cannot respond to Templeton's ideals; he chooses quick cash in the marketplace, as well as the betrayal of honesty and integrity to unfolding wonders of the universe and to fidelity to honor and trust.

Again, Templeton has built his life on a fundamental honesty to what he believes. Even though he becomes known as a satirist through the machinations of his brother Pat, he refuses, because of this honesty, to prostitute his writing and make it grow into something dishonest. He contents himself with writing reviews, a cookbook, and other innocuous publications; foregoes monetary success; becomes in the world's eyes a failure but is in reality a success since he spends his life for others.

As for the duty that keeps him at his wife's side, "The face of the disaster, in spite of its terror for him seemed incalculably noble and austere. He could not have it less than that."[32] The level of what he must give up, both in connection with his wife's need for him and with his refusal to prostitute his writing, has been raised to the ideal; he can do the hard things that life requires because he can see the purpose behind them. Life has meaning, and the meaning enables him to live life well, even though new fashions are overtaking the fundamentals that sustain his outlook.

Alice Brown appears to have captured her own plight in describing that of Templeton; the sound values and high principles of both have become old-fashioned. Undoubtedly, Miss Brown's attempt to bring modernity into her story led her to emphasize the sexual relationship between Irene and Champ and also a curious affair between Elizabeth's mother and Blaisdell, a married man. Just as Elizabeth takes care of the day-to-day needs of Templeton, her mother takes care of the same needs of Blaisdell; just as Elizabeth never had a father's love and substitutes Templeton, her mother never had a husband's love and substitutes Blaisdell.

A review in the *London Times* protested the very subject which became the basis for much later investigation in novels. The review suggests that Templeton is like a Dickens' character and that his wife is like Mrs. Jellyby; Pat and Sally are also worthy of Dickens, but, with them the likeness ends. The review complained that even Dickens at his dullest and most matter-filled "is never dull as the American author of this novel (who has little humor) often is, nor did he overload his books with heavy analysis of emotions. But in nothing is the contrast so great as in the fact that the love that dominates this story is largely illicit— as that of Eunice Hilliard for her chance-married lover and the passion of her daughter Elizabeth for dear Old Templeton—or else a shameless hunting as that of Irene Renfrew. . . ."[33]

Other reviews, however, were not so damning. The *New Republic*, for instance, found that the story "abuses the laws of coincidence and it is often outrageously sentimental, but there is a certain wise tranquility at the core which saves the book from mediocrity."[34] To Grant Overton, the book painted modern relationships between parents and children.[35] "Modern," of course, refers to 1927 modernity, the time when Freudian psychology formed the basis of much literature. Some of these "modern" ideas, however, had not been outmoded; or if they had been discarded, they were again beginning to emerge. Templeton found (together with many modern parents) that his own sway over Sally had simply been allowed to lapse; but if someone had asked him whether he had permitted his control to lapse in "obedience to the rights of youth, tribute to its capacity for judging," he would have uttered a swift denial: "How should they judge, here on a strange planet where they don't know the rules? And if they're expected to bring with them some heavenly sort of intuition, to serve them instead of discipline, you're mistaken. They're just larvae, as their fathers and mothers were before them."[36]

Confronted with Irene's selfish sniveling at feeling sorry for herself in the light of the misery she has caused by her own intemperate behavior, Templeton, in a hard, angry voice asks her what she has to complain about since she is young and has all life before her; but he also tells her that she is a vain little fool who hasn't the vaguest idea about what life means. He says, "You, a small, insignificant atom! you had the power to destroy life, to cause an amount of suffering you couldn't understand to save your soul. . . . Good God! what is the world coming to in the hands of imbeciles like you?" In spite of the cliché, the thought behind his tirade remains a sobering one.

For Templeton, as for Alice Brown, youth must be taught by the wisdom of the mature, and recognition must be made that all the old are not mature. A society that has abdicated its duty to instruct in wisdom reaps its reward in intensified neurotic behavior. On this point, Albert Ellis, the noted psychiatrist, finds that "magazine advertisements, TV dramas, best-selling novels, motion pictures, popular songs and various other popular media" continuously bombard the young person with the "fact" that it will be "terrible if he is unpopular or unloved."[37] And Dr. Ellis adds that schoolchildren and college students "also resist learning new things, changing their behavior. But is this any reason why teachers should stop trying to get them to learn and to change?"[38] Alice Brown applauds the responsibility that must stem from those who teach youth, although she stresses not the unhappiness caused by lack of popularity, lack of affection, but the unhappiness that stems from lack of giving, of loving, of helping, of serving.

Even though the *London Times* accused Miss Brown of lack of humor, *Outlook* found that the novel possessed "abundant grace, charm, understanding, and humor, and we should name it without hesitation as one of the best and most pleasing of Miss Brown's novels."[39] But, whatever the final estimate of *Dear Old Templeton* might be, it indicates Miss Brown's own dilemma. Caught in the first rush of a new outlook that threatened to crush long-cherished ideals, Alice Brown swiftly ranged herself on the side of those attempting to stem the tide; and although she nodded to the new, she never bowed. In her attempt to pour forth the wisdom of her own life (she was sixty years old when *Dear Old Templeton* was published), she filled her story with heavy analysis of emotion, as was noted by the *London Times*; and she gave Templeton so many ideas to expound that she apparently neglected the novelist's task of making her characters plausible. Coincidences do intrude; sentimentality does appear; but the novel—as a vehicle of ideas caught in flux, as an indication of the plight of the novelist herself, as a warning that all too soon became too late—stands as an old-fashioned attempt to carry old-fashioned ideals of honesty, integrity, discipline, duty, and love into a new era. Yet, it would be many years until the admonition to "ask what you can do for your country, not what your country can do for you" would fall on receptive ears. Now, perhaps, as is indicated by widespread disenchantment with what society has made of itself and of its physical world, Alice Brown's ideals and ideas for man to seek man in brotherhood, and for man to seek his physical surroundings in acknowledgment of their beauty and his dependence on them can be considered not outmoded but relevant and necessary to the continued existence of human life.

CHAPTER *6*

Beyond Convention—Later Years

IN his poem "Sanctuary," Lionel Johnson inscribed to
Alice Brown the tribute "Heaven were not heaven and
you not there,"[1] a tribute which might acknowledge that
Alice Brown represents both the ideal and the real in a
superb maturity. Just as heaven is real to her, only through
attention to the ideal can its attainment be realized. The
stories that literally poured from Alice Brown's pen reveal
not only the art the woman formed but also the woman the
art formed. Believing that inspiration "mustn't claim privi-
lege" but must "bend itself humbly to the study of life and
plug away at the artisan side of the task,"[2] Miss Brown confessed that she never had "a purpose, except the purpose
of trying to make a picture of life as it looks to me"; and she
had not "photographed" but had "lived and imagined."[3]

However, an increasing failure to "live" and an increasing
tendency to "imagine" resulted in her neglect to modernize
both her ideas and style—as is clearly indicated in *Dear Old
Templeton*. But the passing of her view of existence and the
coming of another outlook actually began with World War I.
In October, 1917, Montrose J. Moses writes, as a result of an
interview with Miss Brown in Boston, that she was an aloof
sort of person "who takes progress for granted and tries to
let it change her inherited point of view as slightly as possible." He found her, as well as "all literary Boston, sorely
vexed over the difficulties of the world, and trying not to fit
themselves in with the scheme of things, but to fit things in
with the scheme of their inherited standards. It is this the
New England writers are at present concerned about. They
are measuring to see what part world changes are to play in

the general perpetuation of their inherited ideas. . . . These writers are not at all interested in the great facts of life outside the New England village life they know so well."[4]

Montrose Moses correctly attributes the failure of novels such as *The Prisoner* (1916) and *Bromley Neighborhood* (1917) to Miss Brown's attempt to "come to grips with the modern spirit," an attempt she made by trying to fit new moral sentiments into the scheme of things to which she had become accustomed.[5] The novels cited by Moses were selected for analysis because of the time in which they were written, but they were rejected because it was felt that Miss Brown's voice, authentic in using New England as a frame of reference, became distorted when she attempted to amplify this voice in a presentation of sociological, economic, or political problems. Furthermore, Moses finds that Miss Brown's influences are from the past. When he left the interview, she promised to send him something he could use; the essay he received was "Immortality."

Conjecture can be made that Alice Brown's view could not accommodate the subjectivity of the current scene she began to witness. The tragic vision underlying all of her writing simply could not be successfully combined with the Naturalistic technique which emphasized the disorder, rather than the order, of the universe. Yet, if

the naturalistic dramatist is willing to recognize the presence of frustration, conflict, and disorder in the universe—and no one will gainsay him—then he should be willing to look for the presence of 'order, structure, system, form and pattern in the universe.' . . . Speculation is necessary if any intellectual advances are to made, for only thereby can any new perspective be attained. . . . Although it may be unfair to the authors of naturalistic literature to label their work trivial, it does not seem unfair to take note of their limited view. . . . The truly tragic is but one response—albeit the highest—of the spirit to the scenes on the revolving stage.[6]

As the truly tragic is Alice Brown's response, it logically suits a time and section that emphasized "order, structure, system, form, and pattern" rather than "frustration, conflict and disorder." Although the modern world does not lend willing attention to tragedy in the Greek sense,[7] the religious values inherent in tragedy steady the view in the face of every whim and fancy. Alice Brown's values are religious and moral, which attributes hold these values firm:

The principal moral benefit of religion is that it permits a confrontation with the age in which one lives in a perspective which transcends the age and thus puts it in proportion. This both vindicates courage and safeguards against fanaticism. To find courage to do what must be done in a given moment is not the only moral good. It is also very much a moral good that this same moment does not become the be-all and the end-all of one's existence, that in meeting its demands one does not lose the capacity to laugh and to play. One must have experienced the grim humorlessness of contemporary revolutionary ideologies to appreciate fully the humanizing power of the religious perspective.[8]

The difficulty, then, does not appear to stem from the fact that Alice Brown fails to contrast the modern age against the ideals of a previous one, but from the fact that the social problems involved were not her forte; her talent lay elsewhere. The frustration of living in an age one has previously outgrown, coupled with the retrospection of formulated judgments on existence itself, plus the certainty of knowing that the culmination of one's life approaches might naturally result in an emphasis on the mystical and the preternatural, if not the supernatural; and such an emphasis appears in the later work of Alice Brown.

I *Ellen Prior*

Although mysticism appears in many of Alice Brown's earlier stories, it ordinarily takes the form of an unexplained empathy of soul between lovers, or on occasion, particularly in the short stories, the insight which sees the connection between human beings and the life force itself. The mingling of human atoms in this life force (hinted at in *Old Crow*) forms the basis of the mystical-tragic poem *Ellen Prior* (1923), which treats of thwarted affection and its accompanying disillusionment but also shows man and his environment mutually dependent. *Ellen Prior*, which compared favorably with Elizabeth Barrett Browning's *Aurora Leigh*,[9] went through fifteen editions. E. M. Tesslin notes that Miss Brown "displays a lyrical gift with keen analytical faculty . . . not 'Realism' the squalid artificial cult of ugliness à la mode, but Reality, the evocation of lasting beauty from the drama of transitory life."[10] For him, *Ellen Prior* is a soul-drama far more concentrated, impressive, and uplifting than *Aurora Leigh*; for the "promise of permanence is from within; though like all such promises, it remains conditional upon mankind not abdicating the conscious heritage of truth and beauty."[11]

Ellen Prior is driven to her death because of her resolve to allay the sufferings of her blind mother, sufferings caused primarily by Ellen's greedy husband; and Ellen's resolution is reinforced by a wanton's playing upon Ellen's innocence and goodness. "The tale begins with a New England spring,/ A cloud, a breeze, a leaf, a bluebird's wing", when the wild winds shout to laggard springs, "Waste, spill yourself in madness of your flowing,/Rend your own breast in passion of your growing"(2). This wild wind calls also to the human spirit, for wind, wood, leaf, bird—all of nature—surge with life force as human passions overtake the innocence of Ellen Prior when she learns that her handsome, strong, young husband Wayne builds his life on greed and when she believes the story of the wanton Lilla that, because Wayne is evil, Ellen will be parted from him in the afterlife if she herself does not become evil.

To spare her blind mother who is suffering because of Wayne's greed, Ellen takes her out in Lilla's boat, intends to drown her, but instead drowns herself. Lilla desperately tries to save her, not through compassion, but because she believes she would be defying the gods who had willed Ellen's death. Lilla leaves the death boat as a mocking legacy to Wayne, who, in anger and frustration over Ellen's death, slashes the boat to shreds; and unable to bear the calm of the growing trees, he sets the woods that Ellen loved afire. Then, in remorse, he leads Ellen's sightless mother back home. The mother-in-law, for whom he had previously made life miserable, becomes the bearer of two gifts: she wills the coveted land to him; and an even greater gift, she shows him the way to his redemption, so that he ". . . within his house of life alone, Listened a space, trembling, but was not afraid,/ And said her name and Ellen's, and so prayed."(177). Amid the inexorable going and coming of the seasons, the intermingling of all life plays its acts over and over, as the poem concludes:

Enduring, yet hid as a godhead in cloud, in the
dark Woods of Windom,
Life lives, unconsumed, in each root, to the
furthermost thread,
To foam up in yeast of the year, when the new
cup is mingled,
And quicken the dead.(178)

The metaphors flow naturally from the countryside as the connection between life and nature holds firm:

Through mortal joy and pang are mortals made;
Yet still is there some fiercer urge conveyed
Through earth and water, their bright messengers,
The murmurous trees, the wind their leafage stirs.
The child lives not on milk and bread alone
Nor by the fruit of tasks his sires have done
For his inheriting. Though he must eat
Of earth and drink her cup, yet still the sweet
Strong secrecies she stores from hidden stills
Are to his tap.(7)

The mystical union of Ellen Prior with nature, one that Alice Brown herself experienced throughout her life, transcends life on earth. Such unity belongs to a greater reality, one presently being explored by theologians who propose St. Francis of Assisi as the "patron saint of ecologists" in order to combat what is seen as a distortion of Christianity— "a tendency to see God as totally transcendent, or outside the world"—for theologians argue that "the salvation of an individual . . . cannot be dissociated from that of nature itself."[12] *Ellen Prior* images the union of man and man, as well as the interdependency of man and nature; for both man and nature stir with the life force flowing in a universe of beauty and design.

II *Mystical Novels*

The supernatural (or the preternatural) remained ever in Miss Brown's experience. Living the last decades of her life in an old Boston house previously owned by the critic E. P. Whipple, she found the house permeated by his presence. She wrote in a letter to a friend that she would indeed prize Mr. Whipple's portrait, for she knew "the house itself would be glad to have it on its walls. It is a dear comfortable old thing—the house—shabby but loving and quiet—and it has such companionable ghosts!"[13] The "companionable ghosts" were left at times when she vacationed in a house she owned in Newburyport, Massachusetts, and on a farm in Hill, New Hampshire.

As Miss Brown continued to write, her emphasis was more and more on an investigation of things nonphysical, even though she had some correspondence with Esther Bates in which she mentions that she was considering making an "animal film."[14] Other correspondence concerns suggestions made by Oliver Hinsdell about possible filming of *Children of Earth, A Play of New England* and *Pilgrim's Progress;* but Alice Brown, who felt that *Pilgrim's Progress* was "great drama," was not willing to film it.[15] Radio used the short story "A March Wind" from *Tiverton Tales* for a Soconyland Sketch on February 17, 1931 (story adapted by Manley and Carlton). A few years later she wrote in a letter to Esther Bates, "Yes, dear, our world is gone, given over to the troglodytes. I do so much want to interview God, not impertinently but merely interrogative."[16]

The later novels strongly emphasize the mystical. *Kingdom in the Sky* (1932), *Jeremy Hamlin* (1934), and *The Willoughbys* (1935), her last, all mystically explore the afterlife; they interpret man's relationship to God in an attempt to define the connections between the human body and the soul. Even though these novels evince a greater preoccupation with death and the afterlife than the earlier ones (*Kingdom in the Sky,* for instance, has for its setting the place to which its characters are precipitously projected after sudden death in an automobile accident), all of her work, early and late, reveals an attempt to correlate the many facets of being in the individual: the physical (considered the least important), the intellectual (not of much more importance), the emotional (of vast importance), the spiritual (of the greatest importance), and the artistic (in which the emotional and the spiritual blend).

The role of body and soul, always prominent in Miss Brown's explorations, appears to change from her early Deistic vision that is superimposed on a Greek world in which the inexorable laws of existence are paid for by suffering, to her acceptance of the Catholic faith in which suffering becomes necessary to the individual in an Existential climb toward maturity. Her belief in the sanctity of life and in the Godhead as the center of being clearly emerges in a letter of December 28, 1938, to Esther Bates in which she states: "Birth control is, to my mind a horror, heaven-defiling, undercut, vile, as spiritual bad manners as lechery . . . . I think they [Catholics] are nearer seeing birth for what it is! Creation, the mysterious earthly counterfeit of what God does all the time with matter and its life—and I see nothing decent even in anything but a wise chastity when it is necessary even if man—and woman, too—go mad. If we begin—by believing that this earth is *not* 'happy'—it can't be, save by moments—it can't be well fed except in the invisible manner of worship and belief—why that's only a part of it."[17]

Miss Brown's occupation which produced the mystical and otherworld novels in a search for answers to profound questions never ceased. Writing in 1939, she expressed her longing for certainty and her confession that it eluded her: "I yearn toward and worship what is too high for my mind and any man's to reach. And it isn't brought nearer to me by bounding it by words deemed suitable to mortal interpretation."[18] In a later letter, she expresses her dissatisfaction with the myth surrounding many Christian beliefs: "Must you be willing to build the old Christ story on echoes from mythology? Can't His godhead of love and sacrifice stand by itself—or hang by itself on a Cross—without myrmidons of childish legend to guard it round? Can't He have been chosen to live with us in a world of inexorable beauty of law and not man-made miracle?"[19]

III *Acceptance of Catholicism*

But Alice Brown moved toward complete acceptance of Catholicism, a movement apparently started by an unusual friendship with a priest that was engendered through her association as a contributor to the *Commonweal.* Although she never met this priest, a reviewer for *Commonweal,* in person, she corresponded with him from the time of their acquaintance in 1930 until her death in 1948; and in her letters she set her heart on paper. The Alice Brown–Reverend Joseph Mary Lelen letters reveal a woman who apparently became a composite of the idealized woman that Miss Brown created in her stories; for she gave herself spiritually to a love which, for her, transcended space and time. As she held aloft for her heroines a love so pure, so self-effacing, so ecstatic that they failed as flesh-and-blood women if they attained it, she offered this spiritual love to her friend. Since human love was, to her, a manifestation of the Divine, the object of her love was an appropriate one, for to him the spiritual was all important. To him, Alice Brown revealed her religious yearnings as well as her quarrels with organized religion. In 1932 she wrote to him that she "ran from churches because all of them were arrogant in their own certainties, and when they bounded God and defined Him they made Him small—not large—and they took away from his Infinitude, and that hurt me very much."[20]

The correspondence with the Reverend Lelen, carried on in a quavering handwriting, attests to the determination of this lady who published into her ninetieth year. As she considered her letters personal ones to be guarded from alien eyes, she undoubtedly burned the Reverend Lelen's letters to her, just as she burned those of Louise Imogen Guiney. From Miss Brown's letters to him, it may be deduced that she believed he was attempting to convert her to Catholicism, which he evidently was. On September 27, 1931, Sister Mary Augusta wrote the Reverend Lelen in response to his request that she invite Alice Brown to the convent: "On September 15 in response to my pressing invitation, Miss Brown called at the Convent. She is a typical 'Yankee' aristocrat, elegant and charming . . . several times she laughingly referred to herself as a 'heretic.' Like you, Father, I should love to further her entrance into the true fold."[21] Miss Brown did convert to belief in the Catholic faith and actually expressed a desire to be formally received into the Catholic Church.

Reverend Lelen tells the story of this conversion long after Alice Brown's death in a letter of April 6, 1959, to some friends of hers, the Honorable and Mrs. Santen, about a rosary that he had received from Alice Brown, one that had once belonged to Louise Imogen Guiney. The Reverend Lelen writes: "That Rosary may have been the cause of her conversion. When very ill she asked me to go see her and receive her in the Church. She had at last accepted the dogma of the Godhead of Christ."[22] As it was impossible to go himself, the Reverend Lelen wrote to Archbishop Cushing, sent him Alice Brown's letter, and requested that a priest be sent to her. Archbishop Cushing gave both letters to a Reverend Wright, then his vice-chancellor. Two weeks later, in response to a question from Father Lelen as to why a priest had not yet been sent, Archbishop Cushing replied that Reverend Wright had lost the letters but that he would go himself. But by this time it was too late; Alice Brown had died. "Pure, truthful and faithful in her last days,"[23] Alice Brown, although accepting Catholicism, was never formally received into the Catholic Church; undoubtedly, she would have liked it exactly that way.

IV *Life the Final Value*

For Alice Brown, only the "fine deed, the sincere life . . . counts. Nothing else matters. It is a toss-up whether our names are to live or whether they fade out utterly. But if we have fought our good fight, we've had life—all there is in it."[24] Honor, renown, and ceremony did not play a large part in her life. When Mount Holyoke offered her an honorary degree, she was in New Hampshire with a very sick friend in the house, so she wrote them of the circumstances, saying she was "much honored but couldn't possibly go down to take it."[25] The fact that her popularity as a writer diminished and dwindled afforded her amusement rather than anguish, as she writes to Mr. J. T. Babb in January 1942: "I have to be a little amused to see how my stock had gone down in the last years or you would have expended the 2.50 for a 'first' without a qualm."[26]

One of her last letters, one to her friend Esther Bates on May 17, 1948, shortly before her death, reveals Miss Brown's own assessment of the popularity of her work: "The only thing that exists for me now in that line is a little play called *Joint Owners in Spain* which probably lived because it was so well fitted for amateurs."[27] Yet, twenty years later, Clarence Gohdes, an eminent scholar of American literature, chose three volumes of short stories for reprinting because of their "faithful depiction of the New England scene."[28] It is hoped that more of Miss Brown's stories, as well as some of her novels, might have a rebirth. In a letter to Esther Bates, Alice Brown wrote: "But reflect on our *having* in daily life, to go back to Shakespeare for the simplest statements because they are not only more beautiful but simpler and more true than anything else."[29] Some of the statements of Alice Brown might meet the same criteria. An assessment of Alice Brown, poet, dramatist, essayist, biographer, short-story writer, and novelist reveals a competent artist and a remarkable woman. Some of the characteristics that attained her a place in American literature should be considered.

CHAPTER 7

Between Romanticism and Realism

S YLVESTER Baxter's poetic tribute on Alice Brown's
birthday in 1921—"For her's the gift of dreaming true"
—reveals a perception of the technique as well as of the
value of Miss Brown's literary contribution. Imagination informed by the high idealism of a Victorian society formed
the basis of her tales. Beginning under the tenets of
Romanticism, the early novels and short stories reveal
primary emphasis placed on lowly types speaking New
England dialect, with concomitant value of the natural, the
country setting over the artificial, the urban. The importance
of the individual stands forth as problems of life find their
solutions in the healing power of nature, the wisdom of
experience—values which an idealistic society has instilled.
As Realism[1] began to replace Romanticism in American
fiction, Miss Brown attempted to combine some of its tech-
niques with her essentially Romantic gift. Although "Romanticism" sometimes appears as a denigrating term, only
Decadent Romanticism, with its sentimentalizing of the emotion, deserves the denigration. Romanticism as a technique
remains just as valid as Realism; it is merely different.

Alice Brown combines both Romantic and Realistic tech-
niques in her novels, short stories, and plays. The local-
color technique so vividly used in *Tiverton Tales, The
County Road,* and *Country Neighbors,* and the idealism
portrayed in stories in *High Noon* and in *The Day of His
Youth* did not completely disappear from her later novels
such as *John Winterbourne's Family, Old Crow,* and *Dear
Old Templeton.* Even though the problems of life explored
in these novels reach a complexity that refuses to yield to the

simple solutions of a simpler age, the underlying philosophy of an orderly world with its own laws based on a higher sanction than man's never absented itself from Miss Brown's vision. The Romantic emphasis on the individual, as opposed to the group, disappears as Winterbourne, Templeton, and Raven bow gallantly, if not completely willingly, to the pressures of a society they feel they must not renounce. Compromise has overtaken rebellion.

When Alice Brown first received recognition in 1895 for *Meadow-Grass: Tales of New England Life,* Americans still vividly recalled and suffered the aftermath of the Civil War. When her last novel, *The Willoughbys,* was published in 1935, forces were gathering that led to World War II. In between, World War I crosses gave cold evidence of man's continued inhumanity to his own species. During this period, Romanticism as a source of literary inspiration waned; Realism as a literary technique grew; and finally, Naturalism and Existentialism developed, as writers consciously probed their characters' psychological motivations and relationships to an increasingly complex society.[2] When Alice Brown began her life on December 5, 1857, in Hampton Falls, she received as inheritance the blood of generations of New England farmers as well as a more immediate heritage of New England Romanticism[3] and New England Decadent Romanticism;[4] when she died on June 21, 1948, in Boston, she left as her inheritance a vision of a life and a record of a life that might best be described by the words "courage" and "hope."

If one ponders the apparent incongruity between the virtues of courage and hope and the outward events that would seem to belie man's reliance on them, one must recognize that Alice Brown, as a professional writer, wrote because she observed, she felt, she pondered, and she had conclusions to offer. She found, in her observance of the relationships between people, the inspiration upon which to build an image of man and his world that would outlast the accidents of war. When she did pay pen service to World War I, she produced three mediocre novels: *Bromley Neighborhood, The Black Drop,* and *The Wind Between the Worlds.* Decadent Romanticism appears in these as, despite forceful characterizations, the plot tends to melodrama as Miss Brown becomes the patriot ((*The Black Drop* and *Bromley Neighborhood*) and the succorer of the bereaved (*The Wind Between the Worlds*). Clearly, Miss Brown writes her best when defining man's actions as man; for in spite of her amazement at the evil and horror loose in the modern world with its injustices and cruelties, she does not consider man a stoic who must prove his manhood in the defiance of Nietzsche's pit, nor does she find him a stranger who must solace his loneliness in the gratification of animal desires, nor does she adjudge woman a poor cow who must accept the tortures of a universe that batters her bewilderingly and provides no balm for the wounds of living.

If one continues to ponder the incongruity between New England Romanticism and a vision of man and of his life that is psychologically true, one must also recognize that those elements of Romanticism which were used as tools, such as the praise of homely wisdom and the healing power of nature, are not necessarily destructive to art. When science tells one that a carrot may cry in pain as it is cut with a knife, it can be readily imagined that the woods converse with Nick in the novel *Paradise*. The basic need of a human being for an expression of love shows no less truthfully in "Confessions" than in "A Perfect Day for Bananafish," even though the planting of larkspur by Mary's suddenly perceptive husband prevents her pining to death and the failure of Muriel to meet Seymour's need causes his violent act. The old-fashioned may merely be the view from which one approaches the conflict. Miss Brown's approach always remains optimistic.

It would be difficult to find a writer of any era who more distinctly and emphatically repudiates both the Naturalistic and the Atheistic-Existential ideas upon which much current fiction is built—the conclusion that the way life really is really is a rotten joke and that the meaning of life is that there is none—than Alice Brown, who found it "all queer this time of publishers—and authors! translations and the regnancy of Sinclair Lewis, et Al!"[5] For Alice Brown, life did not require a quest for meaning in a meaningless universe; the meaning of life could be read in every mountain and stream, every rock and flower, "And one poor weed, up-springing to the sun / Breeds all creation's wonder, new begun" (*The Road to Castaly*, 4).

Alice Brown saw one world, not because it had to be so considered to prevent a nuclear holocaust, but because it had been created thus. Her world is not only the material universe but a larger reality encompassing that which is beyond and above and better than that which is so naïvely called the "real." This supernatural reality does not wear the covering of religion, or at least of specific religious beliefs; but it presents itself in observable human activity. The words of Pierre Teilhard de Chardin might apply to what Miss Brown sees: "We tend to forget that the supernatural is a leaven, a life principle, not a complete organism. Its purpose is to transform 'nature'; and it cannot do that apart from the material with which nature presents it. . . . The expectation of heaven cannot be kept alive unless it is made flesh. With what body, then, shall our own be clothed? With an immense, *completely human* hope."[6]

This completely human hope informs the novels, the plays, the short stories, and the poetry of Alice Brown. Added to this hope is the admonition to humanity voiced by Lauradel in *The Eighth Day* when she says, "GET LOV-ING, YOU SONS-OF-BITCHES, OR THE WORLD WILL TURN COLD. That's what I sing about! Now do you understand?"[7] Roger Frazier does understand, and so would Alice Brown, although she might shudder at the choice of words. But because the words are different, the message of Thornton Wilder, winner of the National Book Award for 1968 and that of Miss Brown, the winner of the Winthrop Ames prize in 1914, are not necessarily different; for each is based upon compassion for the weak and the unprotected in a world in which men are not good enough because they do not love enough.

As sociology replaces philosophy in the curriculum, as both writer and scientist show how man resembles the animal, some writers, Thornton Wilder and Alice Brown among them, show how man resembles the divine, and thereby they hold out the promise of a better world. For such writers, man—civilized, responsible, and compassionate—heads for an expanding consciousness in an expanding universe, not through drugs but through an apprenticeship in suffering, toward an afterlife that may not be so very different from this one—may even bear some resemblance to one that Alice Brown imagines in *Kingdom in the Sky.* If the imagination rather than a camera records the images in Alice Brown's stories, one must recall the observation of Hermann Hesse that man will see nothing different, no matter how far he explores outer space, for he will see with the same eyes. Although both microscope and imagination reveal views of reality, imagination alone gives order to the observation.

The Romantic technique, then, although perhaps out of date, may actually present a more valid interpretation of experience than the Realistic, the Naturalistic, the Existential—although, indeed, these are not mutually exclusive. Alice Brown, in reflecting her view of reality, writes in the tradition that starts with Homer—in one that recognizes that a literary work becomes a model for, as well as a reflection about, life; that man does indeed live in a society in which the "we" equals in importance the "me"; and that how a man views his world determines to a great extent whether he will grow to the maturity of his potentialities or whether he will wither through neurosis to self-destruction.

Although the "convention of Realism pretended that it was closer to the truth than the conventions of the Gothic novel or of Romance . . . the question should be, to what truth? The novelists who practiced Realism shaped and controlled their worlds, ultimately, in response not to what was out there but to what was inside them."[8] It becomes evident, then, that the lingering Romanticism in the works of Alice Brown does not militate against them; on the contrary, it provides the matter out of which images, as well as ideas, may be formed. In giving credence to that which is experienced emotionally as well as to that which is logically reasoned—more, in emphasizing the emotional over the purely rational—freedom of imagination loosens the restrictions of the purely photographic to result in what is perhaps a more valid way of ordering experience, one way close to that of the tragic vision. The gift of "dreaming true" may best be seen in looking at some of the characters Miss Brown cre-

ates. This necessitates summarizing some of the points previously made in analysis of the various works.

I *Reality*

In writing that Miss Brown "probes the secrets of the
common heart," Gamaliel Bradford poetically recognizes
Alice Brown's ability to characterize, for in her sounding of
the "common" heart she achieves an excellence lacking, in
many instances, in her presentation of more sophisticated
types. Although Henry Walcott Boynton recognizes that for
Miss Brown "rural New England is a scene of more varied
color and contour than for Mrs. Freeman or Mrs. Wharton,"
and although he accords her praise for "fidelity to detail,"
he finds her "essentially romantic": the "neighbors of Bromley are Yankee to the bone, but in the end they have to do
what their literary sponsor's warm fancy demands of them."[9]
It might be remarked that all characters in all authors' stories
suffer the same fate; but more important, the characters who
are "Yankee to the bone" do reveal an authenticity, a way of
relating to the circumstances of their lives which, even
though "Yankee," is also universal. As Alexander Cowie
points out: "Perhaps that is the final responsibility of the
Novelist; he must be true to his times and yet save himself
for Time."[10]

The New England types, such as Farmer Eli and Abigail,
Dilly and Gardener Jim, speak dialect that never falls harsh-
ly on ears unattuned to homely, rural speech. Although Farmer Eli does not soliloquize about his emotions upon
glimpsing the sea for the first time, his actions suit the taciturnity that the reader expects from a man whose life has of
necessity consisted of not much more than daily chores in
back-breaking work. Farmer Eli represents a part of life, and
his reaction to the long-awaited wonder, unexpected though
it might be, brings with it emotional overtones which speak
individually to each reader of the story. Farmer Eli forces
himself into a place in the reader's memory because, as an
individual, he has reacted to the fulfillment of his dream in
an unconventional way; and his reaction forces a heightened awareness which only authenticity brings.

Abigail also remains in the memory as an individual.

Even though her growth from innocence to knowledge of good and evil engages one, Abigail herself clearly emerges as she expertly cracks two eggs together so that her penny-pinching husband will believe that only one egg is going into the cake. Abigail's ability to improvise, as well as her ability to fabricate, helps her to endure what she cannot change (a miserly, interfering husband); but her courage, as well as her love, enables her to change what she need not endure (the miserly, interfering *father*). Even Abigail's husband has touches which lift him from a "type," but Abigail herself emerges clearly and memorable so that an acquaintance with her remains as part of human experience.

Certainly Dilly, the "village witch," is not a type; but she represents many free souls who refuse to be bound by the artificiality of convention. Making her life mainly in the open, enjoying life primarily in its relationship to nature, her homely wisdom of the "do-good" variety may result in solutions to problems that are a bit too pat, but Dilly herself remains an individual who speaks to the depth of the unconscious in the reader. She is able, through her own strength (even though aided by the noninterference of her narrow society) to "do her thing" untrammeled by restricting laws and uncriticized by conventional mores. In Miss Brown's New England, individuals find themselves free to develop their unique propensities without loss of respect for their use of freedom.

Gardener Jim, another individual, although a garden-lover like many, finds solace and salvation in tending gardens. The fact that redemption comes to him does not startle, but that it comes through his avocation permits him to stand out as an individual whose actions carry with them their own, though unforeseen, reward. Even though the solution might appear to be too well-made, Gardener Jim himself, withdrawn, silent, embittered through rejection, remains believable. The list of individuals who are not only plausible as characters but psychologically sound as individuals encompasses almost all of the characters in the New England short stories. Above all, the characters are interesting, varied, and filled with touches that stem from living close to the soil in a society in which the individual counts. Recognition must be given to the fact that difficulties ensue in any attempt to separate characterization from plot in the short story; and, in the sense that they reflect human nature and mirror human actions, all characters are types.

But Alice Brown's memories of rural New England life that form the basis of her stories lend an authenticity resulting in artistic surety. The reader smells the pies baking; his mouth waters when biscuits appear on the table; he warms himself before the ever-present fireplace. The short stories lend themselves to the kind of simple wisdom in which actions carry with them their own punishments or rewards; experience brings knowledge; age instructs youth—more important, youth listens and learns.

Living close to nature, individuals learn many lessons forgotten in urban living—lessons concerning transitory events in juxtaposition to permanent values. In the cycle of the New England seasons, daughters learn that all life has its birth, maturity, and death; that death must precede rebirth; that present life continues what went before and will evolve into future life. Dilly's knowledge of her inheritance in "A Last Assembling" stimulates her to make an unpopular choice—spinsterhood—instead of a rejection of that inheritance. And Miss Brown, spinster herself, finds life valuable as life; its value is not dependent upon such accidentals as marriage and children. False values have no place in an existence wrested from the earth by dint of back-breaking labor.

As Miss Brown's own inheritance of the New England and the literary traditions faded, she attempted portrayal of more sophisticated characters. Although the characters in her novels show higher development and clearer etching, they do not reveal the same authenticity as the characters in the short stories, except when they partake of the same source—Miss Brown's own childhood. Thus Thyrza, a completely believable little girl, turns into a facsimile of a woman: she is shadowy in texture and stilted in speech—a product, apparently, of arrested development. But the fact becomes hard to accept that the highly imaginative, clever, lively little girl did not grow into a better maturity; at least, one is disappointed that so much promise withered unfruitfully. More serious, however, is the conclusion that Miss Brown's art itself withered when she allowed the philosophical statement in the novel to supersede attention to Thyrza's characterization.

When a friend to whom Alice Brown confessed that she should "never cease to regret having no Greek" told her that "writing 'Farmer Eli's Vacation' is better than having Greek, if it couldn't be both," Alice Brown mused that perhaps "what we do easily we don't prize. It's like breathing."[11] The New England tales flowed with great ease from Miss Brown's pen; they have the great art of artlessness. Perhaps this very ease militates against them; for, having produced so many, Miss Brown cannot be singled out for having written a masterpiece, and yet many of the stories could be considered as such. Although there appears a formula—the problem, the insight, the solution—the problems and the solutions are as varied as the flowers described along the way. Miss Brown seems untiring in her inventiveness of plot and character; sometimes she uses the same character at a different point in his or her life to point out the epiphany or to show how men and women become instrumental in furthering their own growth by aiding the growth of others.

Because most of Miss Brown's short stories are really long incidents, it remained for her to use the novels for intricate plot vehicles in which psychological probing of motivations and actions might ride. Even though the early novels do use simple country folk, the main characters ordinarily are well-educated, sophisticated urban people who must battle the encroachment by a demanding society upon their individuality by becoming increasingly materialistic. It appears as though Alice Brown found her inspiration first in a turning back to an earlier day, as in the short stories and early novels, and then attempted to come to grips with the problems newly presented by an expanding technological society. Because she seems to have never really accepted the values of society after World War I, she attempted to present these as problems rather than to create authentic characters. Although the problems are new (at least on the surface), Miss Brown's characters are from a former age; and one is tempted to believe that the problems investigated were Miss Brown's rather than those she observed. The culmination came in *Dear Old Templeton* when the solutions apparently became too difficult to arrive at. After this novel, she took refuge in highly mystical and philosophical novels which almost completely ignored the changes which had occurred in the preceding decades; and, except for a casual mention now and then of automobiles and telephones, the situations, settings, and characters might be from pre-World War I vintage.

Although the novels might be read by the student of sociology as a record of a changing civilization, they are far more important from a literary point of view as examples of universal values that clash with expediency. Although the characters appear to be stereotyped on occasion and although manipulation of plot does occur, the novels, for the most part, manage to hold the reader's interest; for Miss Brown is above all a storyteller; and except for her last three novels, the story carries one along in spite of less than artistic characterization; and even in these last three novels, highly artistic writing intermittently appears. But the permanent value of the novels lies in the philosophic and psychological truth which they reveal and which the reader experiences. Authentic characterizations and psychologically valid actions appear more often in Miss Brown's depiction of the New England common folk in her short stories, than in the protagonists of her novels.

Although Miss Brown has been accused of not being able to depict men, when *My Love and I* was published under the pseudonym of "Martin Redfield," no critical comment appeared to the effect that a woman must have written it; it was accepted as the work of a man. Miss Brown's ability to characterize receives additional notice in a review in the *New York Tribune* which, speaking of *Children of Earth, A Play of New England*, notes that the author has "brought into her lines and characters a ring of truth that is far deeper than photographic Realism, a something resulting from keen insight into the New England heart struggling with a broadly human and vital problem."[12] Even though the novels reveal less art in characterizations than do the short stories, they indicate on the deepest level a universality of theme which attempts to solve the problem of human suffering.

II *Universality*

Gamaliel Bradford recognizes that "what she adores, what she achieves, is truth" in his poetic praise acknowledging the reality of Alice Brown's vision. This reality bases itself on a generally optimistic view of existence, even though "especially since 1920, there has been a gradual increase of pessimism in the American temper."[13] The reason for the general pessimism appears to result from the fact that science and philosophy, as well as war, "have altered the faiths that men lived by. Old standards of value were cast aside, but adequate new ones have not been found—or accepted . . . the dominant note in much modern fiction has been (to use Thomas Wolfe's term) a disturbing 'incertitude'."[14] Alice Brown, like other late-nineteenth-century writers, was of the white-collar class; and as such, she was not really informed concerning the underprivileged masses and their suffering. Even though most writers knew of economic problems, their "point of view was that of the salaried worker, not the wage earner."[15] Added to economic difficulties as a cause of pessimism, the philosophy of scientific determinism, which "swept the intelligensia in the late nineteenth century," negated the rather general assumption that life had a purpose and good would finally prevail, a philosophy that had been of great comfort to the Victorians.[16]

Alice Brown did not embrace the new scientific determinism as a basis of existence; instead, she attempted to formulate answers to problems based on premises above and beyond the present experience. She did not, like so many authors of her times, allow the "editorial arm of fiction [to wither] away, leaving the reader to find his way amid the dispiriting data of the 'Front Page'."[17] Because she did not descend from the heights from which she viewed problems of existence throughout her life, she could obtain a better perspective and a steadiness which saw life whole.

Henry Hartwick, writing in *The Foreground of American Fiction* in 1934, states that novelists "have lagged behind the advances of science, deriving gloomy inferences from outmoded (Newtonian) physics while science has gone on to an 'almost mystical' interpretation of the universe."[18]

Alice Brown, like the scientists, developed an "almost mystical" interpretation of the universe; but in fairness to her, it must be noted that this "almost mystical" interpretation appears in her earliest writings. This interpretation combines visions from Greek tragedy, Christianity, her own experience, and scientific knowledge. Adding an avid interest in the past to her own experience in the present, and giving her life solely to writing, Miss Brown leaves a heritage of fiction psychologically sound in light of present-day knowledge and a way of observing reality optimistically that is founded on courage and hope. As previously noted for Alice Brown, as for Sophocles, Saint Paul, and Teilhard de Chardin, suffering has a purpose because it leads to self-growth which, in turn, leads to love.

That love forms the basis of Alice Brown's writing must be immediately recognized. Her doctrine of love, one continually reiterated, is that love is its own reward. The lover—usually the woman and a willing victim of unrequited love—asks nothing more than service to the beloved; and she happily sublimates her desire for union with the beloved in service either to him or to others. Julie (*Kings End*) finds her happiness in keeping the Judge's death watch; Margaret Warrener finds hers in ministering to her straying husband; Barton Gosse (*The Story of Thyrza*) finds his in writing proposals of marriage to the refusing Thyrza; Martin Redfield (*My Love and I*) finds his in attempting to make his wife happy, as do Winterbourne (*John Winterbourne's Family*) and Templeton (*Dear Old Templeton*). The list could go on and on to include almost every protagonist or important character created by Miss Brown. But underneath this renunciation of the lover lies a larger renunciation: the giving up of one's own selfish goals for unselfish service or duty. And, of extreme importance, the individual who sacrifices self receives his own reward in his growth to maturity as a human being.

Charles Miner Thompson feels that a falsity in Alice Brown's stories "springs partly . . . from the somewhat hysterical way in which she feels her favorite subject: This is the woman whom love has in any way disappointed. Miss Brown is notably occupied with the jilted."[19] Thompson also finds that Miss Brown has a gospel of love "which she preaches continuously. This consolation, this remedy is her personal message to her sex, the great message of her books."[20] The early stories of Alice Brown appear to merit, at least on the surface, Thompson's criticism; but, in the light of her later work, it might be noted that loving, like virtue, is not only its own reward, but also that, through the loving, one becomes more human.

The early stories and novels do not probe deeply into the vital force, love, but they present the results of loving or of not loving. The later novels show a maturity gained, undoubtedly, as much from the earlier writing as from the later living; and this maturity evidences itself in connecting the power and the importance of suffering to the growth of the individual and his ability to help others. For Alice Brown, all men recognize their brotherhood in pain; but for one to give aid and succor to one in grief, he must have experienced suffering himself.

Margaret Warrener can give human comforting because she herself has experienced pain, and she notes that pain is universal: "Everywhere pain is beating on. Uncounted souls suffer and make no sign. The hunger of Heloise, the longing of Tristan, the tragedy of Paolo and Francesca dying in the springtime—these are but legible pages in the book of life. But there are countless pages besides, that no hand has turned. The bird falls in the forest with a wound in his breast. No one knows about the bird. The spent runner drops at his task, and no one cares, save that the message never came. It is everywhere, the universal pang."[21] Twenty years later in *Old Crow*, Alice Brown uses the same idea; but this time she analyzes the meaning of pain in relation to a greater reality. Although suffering abounds throughout the world, and not only man-made suffering, its importance lies in its ability to stimulate human potentialities to their full growth; and part of this growth must result in the knowledge that man is not the measure of all things and that man must finally rely on a power higher than he; for only in recognizing his own humanity can he avoid the pitfalls of arrogance. The dark night of the soul leads, for Alice Brown, through despair to hope.

Closely connected with love and its accompanying suffering is artistic creativity. Born of dissatisfaction, neglectful of creature comforts, the artist must struggle to create. Scarely a novel by Alice Brown fails to contain in a prominent position an artist of some sort, and most of the novels have writers as protagonists. As the interplay of love and creativity through the suffering of renunciation forms the basis of such novels as *My Love and I, Margaret Warrener, Dear Old Templeton,* and *Rose MacLeod,* all solutions to the resulting problems are optimistic. Life, for Alice Brown as for Homer, is living; living, for Alice Brown as for Euripides, is suffering; suffering, for Alice Brown as for Job, is human growth; human growth, for Alice Brown as for Saint Paul, is divine love.

Alice Brown's philosophy insists that man can work through his problems with the help of others, for the world she loves has beauty of order and design. The laws are there for men to live by: love for each other; responsibility for one's family and friends; fidelity to promises made; unselfishness in acceptance of disappointments; kindness and assistance to all in need; honesty in understanding oneself and others. The Judeo-Christian virtues, Alice Brown maintains, lead to the human growth which requires that one become a mature human being before one can grow into faith. That this philosophy found its roots in sincere conviction is demonstrated by the fact that the growth of the protagonists from early novels to late ones parallels Alice Brown's own growth into faith.

III *Form and Content*

Suzanne Alice Roulette, in her poetic tribute to Alice Brown, pinpoints the apparently opposing forces which pull Alice Brown's work toward separate terminals: "Two spirits fine, I think, walk at your side / One bids you to the fair uplands of song / The other leads you on earth's lowly way." The verses might indicate the separation that must be made in considering Alice Brown as literary artist. A natural separation has already been made between her New England tales with their authentic recording of the ways and means of New England life in the late nineteenth and early twentieth centuries and her later novels with their sophisticated characters in urban settings in a more materialistic world. The local-color technique in a Romantic tradition, although used to good advantage by Miss Brown, appears to be insufficient to present the philosophical ideas in the depth to which Miss Brown later aspires. Although homely truths become increasingly important in a society that more and more suffers its own punishment for forgetting them—the destructive force of greed and power; the creative force of empathy and love—the lack of character development which requires probing into motives and actions on all levels of consciousness militates against many of the New England tales, as noted before. In most of them, the motive is too clearly told; the moral is too neatly seen; the point is too easily gained. Even though stories such as "A Day Off," "Farmer Eli's Vacation," and "A Last Assembling" lend themselves to many rereadings for enlargement of understanding, most of the New England stories, although enjoyable, are quickly forgotten.

New England life vividly engraves itself on the reader's memory, however; and, even though characters individually may lose themselves in the numbers of boys and girls, mothers and fathers who lead or are led, come to grief or to joy, the reader enjoys a lasting image of a time when neighbors kindly and helpfully embraced each other in pleasure and sorrow. The picture is of a time when mothers and daughters grew close in knowledge and love; when natural beauties sustained the weary farmer; when clean streams and clear air brought bodily health; when shared ideals and homely virtues brought mental stability. The reader must be grateful to Alice Brown for preserving, not in sentimentality or disdain, but rather in truth and in sympathy, that older, but perhaps saner, manner of life.

The art with which Alice Brown creates this life stems from her knowledge of, and her delight in, the country life which seeped into her being through childhood and girlhood. Her use of the changing seasons to create moods; her contrasts of the bleak aloneness of the winter and the warm companionship of a friendly hearth; her relationships between a garden blossoming in beauty and a love growing in depth—all these not only create subtle atmosphere and tone but also add to the image the oneness of man and nature.

As Alice Brown moved into the portrayal of a later and more complex time, her ability to ask more difficult questions deepened. Although the basis for her ideas did not change, it broadened; and the ideas themselves grew as she developed more complex characters and attempted to solve their problems. As noted, her consideration of problems that stem fundamentally from existence itself caused one of the most serious criticisms of her work. As she developed themes concerned with life on a great, vast scale, the whole Divine Plan as shown in the influence of one individual life upon another came under her scrutiny. Large theories of present existence and life after death led her to create characters who continuously grope for the truth; and this groping leads to long introspective philosophical musings, which, interesting and poetic in themselves, tend to slow the pace of the novel. Some of the novels, therefore, particularly the late ones and in particular *The Willoughbys*, result in philosophical soliloquy rather than in characters in action. Even though many modern novels build themselves on this same technique, Miss Brown's introspection ordinarily concerns the meaning of life itself rather than that of an individual life. Although these passages contain poetry and solace for a perplexed human being attempting to form a philosophy, they require a maturity of outlook and a vividness of imagination beyond that of many readers.

Ample evidence exists that Alice Brown's novels and stories enjoyed extreme popularity in their day. Reviews glow with praise, even though "great" might be too strong an adjective to use. Masterly style and sureness for plot make her a dependable workman. A review in *The New York Times* in 1917 states that she excels in the "rich and glowing interpretation of New England character and temperament" and that she scarcely "has her equal among writers of recent years," finding that "her superiority lies in her power to give the personality all its implications, to interpret it as the creation of heredity and environment, to make it, even mercilessly sometimes, exhibit its inward self down to the last hidden corner of its soul."[22] Other criticism, however, indicates that she sometimes "allows her characters to become too improbable. Usually because of her need for crucial action in the plot."[23]

Such improbability usually does not appear, however, in the New England characters and temperament. Here the art is such that it ordinarily rings true; and when she "drops her sophisticated people, wholesomeness, simplicity, truth, like beautiful children, come flocking as if to welcome a traveler home."[24] The spirit that Suzanne Alice Roulette refers to, then, that leads Alice Brown "on earth's lowly way," apparently directed truly; for many critics feel that the depiction of rural New England characters forms the basis of Miss Brown's excellence as an artist. This is not denied, but as suggested above, presentation of a way of life, imaging of homely virtues, fidelity to wholesome morality—all require less talent than does the attempt to present an artistic work which defines existence itself. In attempting the definition of life, Alice Brown had to be led by the "other" spirit to the "fair uplands of song," and this required a great talent, one greater perhaps than Miss Brown's. The novels, therefore, significant and interesting though they are, lack the same artistic fidelity found in the short stories. If it were possible to combine the artistry of the short stories with the depth of perception in the novels, Alice Brown would reach the highest rung of the ladder of literary eminence.

But as has been constantly observed in this study of Miss Brown, the characters in the novels appear to live mainly to vitalize their author's ideas as they soliloquize, philosophize, and give each other advice about the meaning of life. To present her ideas and her ideals, Miss Brown uses characters in many cases who seem just too good to be true. The normal flaws apparent in humanity do not appear in sufficient light to remove the characters from the realm of high idealization, even though natural and stimulating conversations between them help to maintain plausibility. The ideas that Miss Brown experienced throughout life apparently fascinated her to the extent that they dominated her as she wrote, causing her to lose sight of characterization and plot for pages at a time while exploring ideas that attempt to reach conclusions concerning the source of life and art, that essay

to relate the supernatural and the natural, that try to reach
definite images of the preternatural—all attempts that lead
her into theories that blur, confusing the reader. Undoubtedly her own lack of clarity of foundation as she attempts the
impossible makes for a fraudulence that prevents the reader
from feeling what she attempts to make him feel, the relationship he holds not only with his billions of forebears, but
also the kinship he has with the present natural world.

It appears, then, that Alice Brown, in intellectualizing
experience, falls short of making this experience present to
her readers. In leading the reader to certain conclusions too
obviously, she prevents his reaching his own conclusions in
many cases, thus failing to give him the desire to return
again and again for new insights. It might be said of her as it
has been said of John Phillips Marquand that she tells the
same story over and over again; and even though the story
entertains and enlightens, its sameness palls. The crux of the
matter seems to be that Alice Brown attempts too much,
both in her enormous output and in her commitment to explain existence itself. With a fine talent, a sound philosophy,
an unbounded imagination, and a sincere desire to entertain, she produces novels that fall below the highest level of
achievement primarily because she fails to commit her
talent to a perfection of technique. Her failure to allow her
verbs, for instance, to carry forth her action leads to the lack
of emotional involvement caused by writing "this is this; he
was that; it was when" and so forth; the result is also a
sameness of storytelling in which the reader learns about
what happened instead of feeling himself present at the
happening.

A few novels—notably *Margaret Warrener, John Winterbourne's Family, The Story of Thyrza,* and *Old Crow*—show
fewer of these flaws; for all of the novels analyzed reveal
some of them. The "fair uplands of song" apparently is not
the place in which Miss Brown does her most artistic work.
The groping for words and images to express the meaning
of the universe experienced throughout her own being becomes a task too difficult for her, excellent writer though
she is. The importance of her novels lies, therefore, not in
the artistry of words that produce emotional impact but in

the fundamental truth of a vision that explains life by reference to sound values, an optimism that sees hope even in the evil that men do, a philosophy that merits the applause of the present-day psychologist and scientist alike, and a way of life that young people today experience as saner than the one their parents and grandparents have made.

In summary, the two spirits, then, led her on different paths. The simple, rural New England tales charm with a deceptive simplicity; but they do not attain the depth of the later novels. The novels compel with a philosophical and psychological appeal, but they do not attain the charm of the earlier New England tales. To combine both spirits requires, perhaps, more talent than Miss Brown possesses; the combination requires genius.

CHAPTER *8*

Final Estimate

A^N early work of Alice Brown, *Mercy Warren* (1896) reveals that Miss Brown finds in Mercy Warren not only a
kindred spirit but one who adhered to her own high ideals.
In painting Mercy Warren and other American Revolution-
ists, she paints herself: "One spiritual grace possessed in
great measure by these stern-fibred men and women was a
serenity of faith in 'final good.' For them there was no whining pessimism. They had mounted far enough, not to lose
sight of the clouds, but to know they lay below."[1] As Mercy
Warren "had determined to have no shackles on her mind
and spirit . . . would grow while life was left her,"[2] so also
did Alice Brown. Mercy Warren lived to the age of eighty-
six; Alice Brown lived to ninety, and she grew "while life
was left her."

If the formal term "religion" can be applied to the unfor-
malized beliefs[3] that provide the framework for Alice
Brown's works and her life, her religion consists of an optimistic belief that the good life can be obtained by faithful
adherence to high ideals of love; that the progress of mankind will be determined by the measure of its faithfulness to
these ideals; and that natural man, in love with nature and
nature's God, will be led to his highest maturity through
love for his fellow man. She not only imaged this creed in
her stories, but also founded a happy and successful life on
it. As pointed out again and again, courage and hope are the
most marked qualities of her life as they are the most
marked ones of the characters in her novels and short stories,
her plays and her poetry. She would have wished nothing

better than to instill some of this courage and hope into a
generation that has not tasted much of either.

The growth to maturity of the little Hampton Falls girl
who "escaped to Boston where books were written" came
through adherence to traditional values—particularly as
Agnes Repplier says, to "the creed of confidence and courage."[4] The optimistic view of the universe revealed in her
writing reflects fundamentally her own experience. With so
much beauty to be enjoyed, with so many miracles of nature
to heal, with wondrous poetry to solace, with a wealth of
words to enchant—how could anyone be pessimistic? As
she writes in *Bromley Neighborhood:* "The moral code
. . . is, after all, the code of truth and beauty. What you
think every day gets its reward in what you do on a day when
your need is greatest."[5]

That Alice Brown's everyday thoughts encompassed the
code of truth and beauty appears evident throughout her
writings. And the rewards of the thoughts that had gone into
her own making came increasingly as she became able to
live in contentment and to write without ceasing until the
end of her life. As she had lived under her moral code of
beauty and truth and as she poured forth her own convic-
tions in attempting solutions of universal problems, her reward became not only an identification with the heroines
she had created but a knowledge that in creating these heroines she had created herself. As she reached out to the Reverend Joseph Mary Lelen in outpourings of love, she became her heroines from Margaret Warrener to Ellen Prior
and beyond, who offered the sacrifice of present joy for a
spiritualized romance that should have its consummation
beyond threat of physical infirmity or mental impediment,
to dwell forever in a heavenly kingdom. Like Bunyan's
Christian to his wife, she held out her arms to the Reverend
Lelen and whispered, "Come, come."

The year before her death, the Reverend Francis Sweeney
went to see her in connection with some of her letters in
the Louise Imogen Guiney Room at the College of the Holy
Cross. He found Alice Brown a white-haired, smooth-faced
little old lady, quite deaf, but with a voice as clear as a bell.
She proposed a toast to her own death and homecoming in

heaven. For the Reverend Sweeney, "so much courage and hope were in the words" that he raised his glass "with a prayer for the uncovenanted mercies."[6] Alice Brown died in Boston on June 21, 1948; but she had been ready to die for a long time, as she wrote to the Reverend Lelen in 1944: "Yes, I think we shall all be glad to go, no matter how 'charged with punishment the scroll.' The day's work will at least be done."[7]

Alice Brown's "day's work" was well done, as evidenced by the wealth of observing, wondering, writing, and living she accomplished throughout her life which she left as an American cultural heritage. Her New England countryside blooms with beauty and peace, old-fashioned virtues support lives of dignity and service, courage and hope defy the purveyors of cowardice and pessimism. This heritage, which she had received from her ancestors, she transmitted, brightly polished, to her readers. For Alice Brown, to live life with love of one's fellows and with appreciation of the natural was all. For the living of it, she was both interpreter and model: and no finer accolade exists.

Notes and References

Chapter One

1. While Alice Brown was president of the Boston Authors' Club (1920–23), literary friends contributed a madrigal of verses in her honor on her sixty-fourth birthday, December 5, 1921. These hand-written accolades, which appear in text of each chapter, are preserved in the Boston Public Library.

2. Max J. Herzberg, ed., *The Reader's Encyclopedia of American Literature* (New York, 1964), p. 114.

3. Fred Lewis Pattee, *History of American Literature Since 1870* (New York, 1915), p. 241.

4. Honorable Warren Brown, *History of Hampton Falls, New Hampshire* (Concord, New Hampshire, 1918), p. 277.

5. "Alice Brown," *Alice Brown* (New York, n.d.), p. 4. This pamphlet was published by the Macmillan Company, Miss Brown's publishers, shortly after the publication in 1927 of *Dear Old Templeton*. It contains a short autobiographical sketch, some biographical information, and a few short excerpts from reviews. Parts are anonymous. Copy of this pamphlet is available in the Boston Athenaeum.

6. On the occasion of the present writer's visit to Hampton Falls, the town hall was closed because of the vacation of the town clerk. When I later addressed a letter to the town clerk (who, I was informed, was the wife of the postmaster) requesting some information regarding early records of Alice Brown and her family, I received no reply.

7. Alice Brown, "The Author of *Dear Old Templeton* Interviews Herself," *Alice Brown*, p. 4.

8. Blanche Colton Williams, *Our Short Story Writers* (New York, 1926), p. 3.

9. Neither the schoolhouse nor Robinson Seminary remains standing. Hampton Falls looks at present much as it must have looked when Alice Brown lived there, with the addition of a few modern homes. A small library stands across from the town hall at a crossroads in the midst of several residences. The library opens for a few hours on two afternoons a week. To this library Alice

Brown left her personal collection of books. During a visit, the present writer was able to purchase a library discard of one of these books, one containing her autograph, for ten cents.

10. Alice Brown, "The Author of *Dear Old Templeton* Interviews Herself," p. 6.

11. Miss Brown evidently admired larkspur above all other flowers, for she mentions it particularly time and time again. For instance, a bed of larkspur literally saves Mary's life in the short story "Confessions," for her husband's planting of a bed of it gives Mary evidence of his love and concern for her, a love and concern he had found impossible to put into words. Further, in reply to a letter from her friend Alice Tallant about "spring fever," Alice Brown confesses that she spends most of her *real* energy thinking about phlox and larkspur. (Letter written probably in 1907 is in Sophia Smith Collection at Smith College.) Again, in a letter dated July 7 (no year) to the Reverend Joseph Mary Lelen (1873–1964) of the Glenmary Missions, Glendale, Ohio, she writes: "And let me tell you, too, what a miracle I found in my room—the miracle of the larkspur. There have been stalks of it on a dark table for days, and now the wonder I have been waiting for has been accomplished. I always keep larkspur and roses until their petals are shed at their feet—and last night it happened. The table, the floor, are blue with the exquisite blue of beauty transformed—flowers changed into translucent gems." (Letter is in unpublished collection in Louise Imogen Guiney Room, Dinand Library, College of the Holy Cross, Worcester, Massachusetts. All letters from Alice Brown to the Reverend Joseph M. Lelen cited in this work are also in this collection.)

12. Williams, *Our Short Story Writers*, pp. 7–8.

13. *John Winterbourne's Family* (Boston and New York, 1910), p. 310

14. *Rose MacLeod* (Boston and New York, 1908), p. 80.

15. In the letter to Alice Tallant referred to in 11 above, Miss Brown writes that "the spring *does* put something into us, doesn't it? Or it stirs something and the sap in us mounts with the blood of the leaf. I'll tell you what I think—it's better to ache and be homesick for the loveliness we love than to settle into too dull a clam! Let's ache."

16. Harriet Prescott Spofford, "Alice Brown," *Book Buyer*, XIII 1896), 636.

17. Alice Brown, unpublished letter to Sister Clarissa, July 26, 1931. (Letter is in present writer's collection.)

18. Alice Brown, "The Author of *Dear Old Templeton* Interviews Herself," pp. 6–7.

19. Alice Brown's letters give evidence that she often did the daring thing. She delighted in being called "Tiger" by her friends, evidently feeling that it suited her, while being described as a "sweet old lady" afforded her much glee. In an unpublished letter to the Reverend Lelen, September 18, 1931, she writes: "I found more people saw and liked the wild, untamed me inside me than I had guessed. . . . There *is* a wild me in me, but it crouches by your side and loves your careless hand on its head while you smoke and read."

20. A complete file of the *Christian Register* dating from 1821 is on hand at the office of the Unitarian Universalist Association, 28 Beacon Street, Boston. *The Christian Register* became *The Unitarian Register* about 1954 "amidst some of the hottest theological arguments since Cotton Mather," according to an unpublished letter to the present writer from Edward Darling, editor of the *Unitarian Universalist World* (March 15, 1970). In 1961 it had become *The Unitarian-Universalist Register-Leader,* but as of March 1, 1970, it is a tabloid newspaper, issued every two weeks, under the name of *Unitarian Universalist World,* having a paid circulation for the newspaper of 82,000; previous high was 12,500.

21. This magazine, originally founded for young people by Nathaniel Willis and Asa Rand in Boston in April, 1827, began with a circulation of several thousand and numbered a half million subscribers by 1899, having become, in 1857, a magazine for adults as well as for children. Some distinguished contributors were Harriet Beecher Stowe, Alfred Lord Tennyson, John Greenleaf Whittier, William Dean Howells, Jules Verne, and Jack London. It merged in 1929 with *The American Boy* and ceased publication in 1941. An anthology, *Youth's Companion,* was compiled in 1954 by four of its former editors.

22. Fred Lewis Pattee, *The New American Literature* (New York, 1930), p. 316.

23. Della MacLeod, *The New York Press,* January 10, 1915, p. 4.

24. Fred Lewis Pattee, *The New American Literature* p. 316.

25. *Ibid.,* p. 317.

26. Francis A. Sweeney, "Friend of Lou Guiney's," *America,* Vol. 80 (Feb. 1949), p. 546.

27. *By Oak and Thorn* (Boston and New York, 1896), p. 209.

28. The Women's Rest Tour Association, founded in 1891, is still in existence, with office at 264 Boylston Street, Boston. Founded primarily to meet the need of women traveling alone, it furnishes lodging lists to members, which lists are supplied by other members from firsthand knowledge, in the interest of safety and economy. *Pilgrim Scrip,* first issued in November, 1892, contains

travel articles, advice, and miscellaneous information for the benefit of the traveler, all supplied by members of the Association.
Pilgrim Scrip is still issued, biannually, together with a Lodging
List. The first president of the Association was Mrs. Julia Howe,
who served from 1891 to 1910; the next was Alice Brown, who
served from 1911 until her death in 1948. An interesting note appears in a pamphlet prepared by the Association (*circa* 1967) regarding Alice Brown's presidency: "The high standards in matters
of diction that she set and insisted upon from the beginning were
never relaxed. Everything emanating from the society, even routine announcements, was submitted for her approval before being
sent to the printer."

29. Sweeney, p. 546.

30. Alice Brown, unpublished letter to Alice Tallant, 1947. (Letter
is in collection at Smith College.)

31. Alice Brown, unpublished letter to Alice Tallant, August 15,
1896. (Letter is in collection at Smith College.)

32. *Three Heroines of New England Romance* (Boston, 1894),
frontpiece.

33. Fred Lewis Pattee, *History of American Literature Since
1870*, p. 241.

34. Susan Erickson Allen Toth, "More than Local-Color: A Reappraisal of Rose Terry Cooke, Mary Wilkins Freeman and Alice
Brown" (unpublished doctoral dissertation, University of Minnesota, 1969), p. 256.

35. *The Whole Family* (A novel by twelve authors—William Dean
Howells, Mary E. Wilkins Freeman, John Kendrick Bangs, Mary
Raymond Shipman Andrews, Mary Stewart Cutting, Alice Brown,
Henry Van Dyke, Elizabeth Stuart Phelps, Elizabeth Jordan, Edith
Wyatt, Mary Heaton Vorse, Henry James). (New York, 1908.)

Chapter Two

1. Louise Imogen Guiney, unpublished letter to Sarah Orne
Jewett, December 30, no year. (In Boston Public Library).

2. "Country Neighbors," *North American Review*, CXCII
(November, 1910), 13.

3. Grant Overton, *The Women Who Make Our Novels* (New York,
1922), p. 13.

4. Toth, p. 256.

5. Alexander Cowie, *The Rise of the American Novel* (New York,
1951), pp. 536—37.

6. *Ibid.*

7. Harry R. Warfel and G. Harrison Orians (eds.). *American Local-Color Stories* (New York, 1941), p. x.

8. *Ibid.*, p. xxiii.

9. Cowie, p. 749.

10. Warfel and Orians (eds.), p. x.

11. Toth, p. 259.

12. *Ibid.*

13. Alice Brown, unpublished letter to Gamaliel Bradford, October 28, 1921. (Letter is in collection at Houghton Library, Harvard University.)

14. "English Folk-Tales," *The Book Buyer*, XIII (November, 1896), 651.

15. Horace Scudder, "Half a Dozen Story-Books," *The Atlantic Monthly*, LXXVI (October, 1895), 559.

16. Gordon Rattray Taylor, *The Biological Time Bomb* (New York, 1968), p. 177.

17. *Ibid.*

18. "Farmer Eli's Vacation," *Meadow-Grass: Tales of New England Life* (Boston, 1895), pp. 19—20.

19. *Ibid.*, p. 26.

20. *Ibid.*, p. 28.

21. *Ibid.*, p. 29.

22. "At Sudleigh Fair," *Meadow-Grass*, pp. 192—93.

23. *Ibid.*, p. 205.

24. *Ibid.*, p. 199.

25. *Ibid.*, p. 226.

26. *Ibid.*, pp. 227–28.

27. *Ibid.*, p. 200

28. *Ibid.*, p. 227.

29. Joost A. M. Meerloo, M.D., Ph.D., *Suicide and Mass Suicide* (New York, 1962), p. 135.

30. "A Righteous Bargain," *Meadow-Grass*, p. 140.

31. *Ibid.*, p. 156.

32. *Ibid.*, p. 164.

33. "To M.G.R." is one of the rare dedications of Miss Brown. Outside of dedicating *Children of Earth* to Winthrop Ames and a few nonfiction books to Louise Imogen Guiney, she used no personal names to link her publicly with her friends. The fact that only initials are used in this case attests to her desire to keep personal and professional life separate.

34. Peter L. Berger, *A Rumor of Angels* (New York, 1969), p. 121.

35. "Dooryards," *Tiverton Tales* (Ridgewood, New Jersey, 1967), p. 8.

36. *Ibid.*, p. 9.

37. "The End of All Living," *Tiverton Tales*, pp. 338–39.

38. "Horn O' the Moon," *Tiverton Tales*, p. 128.

39. "A Last Assembling," *Tiverton Tales*, p. 153.

40. *Ibid.*, p. 154.

41. *Ibid.*, p. 166.

42. *Ibid.*, p. 169.

43. *Ibid.*, pp. 169–70.

44. *Ibid.*, pp. 170–71.

45. *Ibid.*, p. 174.

46. "A Second Marriage," *Tiverton Tales*, p. 254.

47. *Ibid.*, p. 261.

48. *Ibid.*, p. 262.

49. *Ibid.*, pp. 245–46.

50. "A Day Off," *The County Road* (Ridgewood, New Jersey, 1968), p. 12.

51. *Ibid.*, p. 14.

52. *Ibid.*, p. 21.

53. "A Winter's Courting," *The County Road*, p. 104.

54. *Ibid.*, p. 111.

55. "A Sea Change," *The County Road*, p. 163.

56. *Ibid.*, p. 165.

57. "A Poetess in Spring," *Country Neighbors* (Boston and New York, 1910), p. 329.

58. "A Flower of April," *Country Neighbors*, p. 43.

59. *Ibid.*, p. 52.

60. "Gardener Jim," *Country Neighbors*, p. 209.

61. "The Other Mrs. Dill," *Country Neighbors*, pp. 250–51.

62. *Ibid.*, p. 261.

63. See Caroline Bird (with Sara Welles Briller), *Born Female*, Pocket Books (New York, 1969), page 127 of which reads: "Women are still expected to work for men, to make life 'sweet and agreeable' for them at home and now at work. . . . But never for herself first. Never for personal power or prestige." See also Betty Friedan, *The Feminine Mystique*, (New York, 1963) (reprinted by Dell Publishing Co., Inc., 1970).

64. Charles Miner Thompson, "The Short Stories of Alice Brown," *The Atlantic Monthly*, XCVIII (July, 1906), 56.

65. "His Enemy," *High Noon*, (Boston and New York, 1904), p. 128.

66. "A Meeting in the Market Place," *High Noon*, p. 9.

67. *Ibid.*, pp. 11–12.

68. *Ibid.*, p. 23.

69. "The Book of Love," *High Noon*, p. 32.

70. *Ibid.*, pp. 38–39.

71. *Ibid.*, p. 61.

72. *Ibid.*, p. 44.

73. "Rosamund in Heaven," *High Noon*, p. 185.

74. *Ibid.*, p. 187.

75. Alice Brown, unpublished letter to Reverend Joseph M. Lelen, April 10, 1931.

76. Alice Brown, unpublished letter to Reverend Joseph M. Lelen, May 7, 1931.

77. Review of *High Noon*, *The Nation*, LXXVIII (May 17, 1904), 395—96.

78. Thornton Wilder, unpublished letter to present writer, March 17, 1969.

79. Alice Brown, *The Day of His Youth* (Boston and New York, 1897), pp. 117—18.

Chapter Three

1. *Alice Brown*, p. 7.

2. Review, *The Herald*, June 1, 1914. (This and other reviews and news items of *Children of Earth* quoted in this chapter are available in Scrapbook, Winthrop Ames Collection, Library of Lincoln Center for the Performing Arts, New York.)

3. Review, *The Boston Transcript*, January 13, 1915.

4. Review, *The New York Tribune*, January 13, 1915.

5. Review, *The Dial*, January 13, 1915.

6. Review, The *Times*, January 13, 1915.

7. "Current Attractions," *Evening Sun*, January 23, 1915.

8. Burns Mantle, Review, *Evening Mail*, January 22, 1915.

9. *Journal of Commerce*, January 23, 1915.

10. *Telegraph*, January 28, 1915.

11. *Alice Brown*, p. 7.

12. Louis Sherman, "The Passing Show," *Evening Globe*, January 23, 1915.

13. *Children of Earth, A Play of New England* (New York, 1915), p. 28.

14. *Ibid.*, p. 24.

15. *Ibid.*, p. 41.

16. *Ibid.*, p. 8.

17. *Ibid.*, p. 208.

18. In a letter to the Reverend Lelen, which she asks him to "please burn," Alice Brown indicates that a friend of hers is "different" and adds that "some women are not meant for motherhood."

19. The distinction between "tragedy" and "comedy" used here is based upon the happy ending of comedy in which multitudinous

lines of plot work out optimistically, while the ending of tragedy involves unhappy destruction, even though wisdom is gained.

20. Review, *The Herald*, June 1, 1914.

21. "The Web," *One-Act Plays* (New York, 1921), p. 129.

22. *Ibid.*, p. 130.

23. *Ibid.*

24. *Alice Brown*, p. 10.

25. While the present writer was visiting Hampton Falls in search of the atmosphere that fashioned Alice Brown's early life, a resident of Kensington (the neighboring town), the Reverend Roland. Sawyer, a retired minister aged ninety-four, conducted a tour of the surrounding neighborhood. He explained that a certain house, which he pointed out and which stood alongside the road, had been occupied by two sisters who, after a severe quarrel, had divided the house right down the middle with a piece of chalk, each one respecting the privacy and ownership of the other "even down to the fireplace." Undoubtedly, the knowledge of the life of these near neighbors gave Alice Brown her solution to the problem of Miss Dyer and Mrs. Blair.

26. "Joint Owners in Spain," *One-Act Plays*, p. 163.

27. *Ibid.*, p. 175.

28. Edwin Clark, Review, *New York Times*, January 25, 1925, Sec. III, p. 16.

29. "Preface," *Charles Lamb, A Play* (New York, 1924), p. x.

30. One of Alice Brown's later novels, *The Kingdom in the Sky,* purports to tell "what might befall us when we leave this scene of our conflict and our nostalgia, for some not too remote and kindly refuge after death," (Foreword, *The Kingdom in the Sky* [Norwood, Massachusetts, 1932], p. v). The novel concerns the afterlives of a group of people killed in an automobile accident. Furthermore, in a letter to the Reverend Lelen (August 17, 1932), Miss Brown writes: "I'm pretty childlike about a tangible world to come."

31. *Pilgrim's Progress* (Boston, 1944), p. 98.

32. *Pilgrim's Progress*, p. 39.

33. *Ibid.*, p. 49.

34. *Ibid.*, p. 95.

Chapter Four

1. Alice Brown, unpublished letter to Reverend Joseph M. Lelen, April 10, 1931.

2. Irene Samuel, *Dante and Milton* (Ithaca, New York; 1966), p. 65.

3. *Ibid.*, p. 158.

4. *Ibid.*, p. 162.

5. "A New England Poet," *The Seminarian* (Exeter, New Hampshire), I (June, 1915), 5.

6. Max J. Herzberg (ed.), "Frost, Robert Lee," *The Reader's Encyclopedia of American Literature*, p. 363.

7. *My Love and I* (New York, 1912), p. 3.

8. *Ibid.*, p. 17.

9. *Ibid.*, p. 34.

10. *Ibid.*, p. 376.

11. *Ibid.*, p. 377.

12. *Ibid.*, p. 285.

13. *Ibid.*, p. 60.

14. *Ibid.*, p. 61.

15. *Ibid.*, p. 375.

16. Karen Horney, M.D., *Feminine Psychology* (New York, 1967), p. 242, quoted from "The Neurotic Need for Love" (lecture given at the meeting of the Deutsche Psychoanalytische Gesellschaft, December 23, 1936, "Das neurotische Liebesbedurfnis," Zentralbl. f. Psychother., pp. 69—82).

17. *Margaret Warrener* (Boston, 1901), p. 36.

18. *Ibid.*, p. 153.

19. *Ibid.*, p. 381.

20. *Ibid.*, p. 498.

21. *Ibid.*, p. 499.

22. *Ibid.*, p. 501.

23. Flora Mai Holly, "Review—*Margaret Warrener*," *The Bookman*, XV (March, 1902), 105.

24. *Margaret Warrener*, pp. 109—10.

25. *Ibid.*, p. 287.

26. Louis Bredvold, "The Modern Temper and Tragic Drama," in *Tragedy: Modern Essays in Criticism*, eds. L. Michel and R. Sewall (Englewood Cliffs, New Jersey; 1963), p. 339.

27. *Kings End* (Boston, 1901), p. 50.

28. *Ibid.*, p. 141.

29. *Ibid.*, p. 207.

30. *Ibid.*, p. 174.

31. *Ibid.*, p. 82.

32. *Ibid.*, p. 81.

33. *Ibid.*, p. 240.

34. *Ibid.*, p. 246.

35. Alice Brown, unpublished letter to Reverend Joseph M. Lelen, May 4, 1931.

36. In a letter to the Reverend Lelen, April 10, 1931, Alice Brown

writes: "And anyway we want to be only what we *are* to be. I could be a little weed for God to set his foot on in His garden."

37. *Old Crow* (New York, 1922), p. 33.
38. *Ibid.*, p. 48.
39. *Ibid.*, p. 55.
40. *Ibid.*, p. 84.
41. *Ibid.*, p. 528.
42. *Ibid.*, p. 264.
43. *Ibid.*, p. 265.
44. *Ibid.*, p. 465.
45. Albert Ellis, *Reason and Emotion in Psychotherapy* (New York, 1963), p. 415.
46. *Alice Brown*, p. 12.

Chapter Five

1. Mary Ford, "A New Character in Fiction," *The Forum*, XL (August, 1908), p. 132.
2. Ward Clark, "Miss Brown's *Rose MacLeod*," *The Bookman*, XXVII (July, 1908), p. 494.
3. *Rose MacLeod*, p. 294.
4. Mary Ford, p. 132.
5. *Ibid.*
6. "Sorting the Seeds," *The Atlantic Monthly*, CIII (May, 1909), 710 [unsigned review].
7. Review, *The Independent*, LXVI (April 15, 1909), pp. 812–13.
8. *The Story of Thyrza* (Boston and New York, 1909), p. 29.
9. *Ibid.*, p. 13.
10. *Ibid.*, p. 120.
11. *Ibid.*, p. 114.
12. *Ibid.*, p. 178.
13. *Ibid.*, p. 284.
14. *Ibid.*, p. 289.
15. *Ibid.*, p. 298.
16. *Ibid.*, p. 315.
17. *Ibid.*, p. 313.
18. *Ibid.*, p. 326.
19. Margaret Sherwood, "Lying Like Truth," *The Atlantic Monthly*, X (December, 1910), 807.
20. Alice Brown, *John Winterbourne's Family*, p. 37.
21. *Ibid.*, p. 298.
22. *Ibid.*, p. 316.

23. *Ibid.*, p. 298.

24. *Ibid.*, p. 345.

25. *Ibid.*, p. 416.

26. *Ibid.*, p. 316.

27. *Ibid.*, p. 389.

28. "A Guide to the New Books," *The Literary Digest*, XLI (November 5, 1910), 814.

29. *Dear Old Templeton* (New York, 1927), p. 327.

30. *Ibid.*, p. 184.

31. *Ibid.*, pp. 220–21.

32. *Ibid.*, p. 386.

33. Review, *London Times* (Literary Supplement), September 15, 1927, 625.

34. E.H.W., "Review," *The New Republic*, LI (July 20, 1927), 236.

35. Grant Overton, "Dear Old Templeton," *Mentor*, XV (September, 1927), 58.

36. *Dear Old Templeton*, p. 409.

37. Albert Ellis, *Reason and Emotion in Psychotherapy*, p. 192.

38. *Ibid.*, p. 194.

39. Review, *Outlook*, July 6, 1927, p. 322.

Chapter Six

1. This comment appears in an unpublished note written by the Reverend Lelen in archives of College of the Holy Cross.

2. *Alice Brown*, p. 3.

3. *Ibid., passim.*

4. Montrose J. Moses, "Miss Alice Brown's Inheritance," *The Book News Monthly*, XXXV, 2 (October, 1917), p. 37.

5. *Ibid.*

6. William Van O'Connor, *Climates of Tragedy* (New York, 1965), pp. 87–89.

7. "Tragedy" is used here to mean the inexorable working out of orderly processes, action and reaction, in the universe.

8. Berger, p. 121.

9. E.M. Tessim, *Poetry Review*, VII (April, 1924), p. 114.

10. *Ibid.*, p. 113.

11. *Ibid.*, p. 114.

12. Edward B. Fiske, "Religion," *The New York Times*, Sunday, January 4, 1970, p. 7E.

13. Alice Brown, unpublished letter to Miss Whiting, March 1 (believed to be 1921). Letter is at Boston Public Library.

14. Alice Brown, unpublished letter to Esther Bates, no date. (Unpublished letters from Alice Brown to Esther Bates cited in this chapter are in the Yale University Library.)

15. Alice Brown, unpublished letters to Esther Bates, April 28, 1940, and May 6, 1940.

16. Alice Brown, unpublished letter to Esther Bates, April 2 (*circa* 1938).

17. Alice Brown, unpublished letter to Esther Bates, December 28, 1938.

18. Alice Brown, unpublished letter to the Reverend Lelen, July 12, 1939.

19. Alice Brown, unpublished letter to the Reverend Lelen, July 13, 1939.

20. Alice Brown, unpublished letter to the Reverend Lelen, August 17, 1932.

21. Sister Mary Augusta, unpublished letter to the Reverend Lelen, September 27, 1931. (Letter is in Louise Imogen Guiney Room, College of the Holy Cross.)

22. The Reverend Lelen, unpublished letter to the Honorable and Mrs. Santen, April 6, 1959. (Letter is in Louise Imogen Guiney Room, College of the Holy Cross.)

23. *Ibid*

24. "A New England Poet," p. 8.

25. Alice Brown, unpublished letter to the Reverend Lelen, July 12, 1939.

26. Alice Brown, unpublished letter to Mr. J. T. Babb, January 19, 1942. (Letter is in Yale University Library.)

27. Alice Brown, unpublished letter to Esther Bates, May 17, 1948.

28. Dr. Clarence Gohdes selected *Tiverton Tiles* and *The County Road* for republication.

29. Alice Brown, unpublished letter to Esther Bates (circa 1938).

Chapter Seven

1. George Levine defines "Realism" in "Realism, or in Praise of Lying: Some Nineteenth Century Novels," *College English*, XXI, 4 (January, 1970), 356. He states that the "world of the 'realistic' novel is one in which characters cannot shape their fates, but must learn to accommodate themselves to the world's pressures." In this sense the word is used in this chapter.

2. Of course, many factors were at work during this period, such as French, Russian, and other foreign influences; scientific in-

fluences, e.g. Darwinianism; the development of psychoanalysis. I focus, however, only on the phases most appropriate to an understanding of Alice Brown's work.

3. "New England Romanticism" is here used to mean the literary technique which uses (a) local color, (b) the lower classes, (c) importance of nature, (d) emphasis on the individual.

4. "New England Decadent Romanticism" is here used to mean the sentimentalizing of the aspects mentioned in note 3 above.

5. Alice Brown, unpublished letter to the Reverend Lelen, May 23, 1933.

6. Pierre Teilhard de Chardin, *Hymn of the Universe* (New York, 1961), pp. 111–12.

7. Thornton Wilder, *The Eighth Day* (New York, 1967), p. 255.

8. George Levine, p. 363.

9. Henry Walcott Boynton, "Some Stories of the Month," *Bookman*, XLVI (September, 1917), 95.

10. Cowie, p. 754.

11. Alice Brown, unpublished letter to the Reverend Lelen, September 18, 1931.

12. New York *Tribune*, January 13, 1915.

13. Cowie, p. 743.

14. *Ibid.*

15. *Ibid.*, p. 744.

16. *Ibid.*, p. 748.

17. *Ibid.*, p. 749.

18. Henry Hartwick, *The Foreground of American Fiction* (New York, 1934), p. 13 (as quoted by Alexander Cowie in *The Rise of the American Novel*, p. 749).

19. Charles Miner Thompson, pp. 57–58.

20. *Ibid.*, p. 58.

21. *Margaret Warrener*, p. 312.

22. "Book Review," *The New York Times*, July 8, 1917, p. 255.

23. *Ibid.*

24. Charles Miner Thompson, p. 61.

Chapter Eight

1. *Mercy Warren* (New York, 1896), p. 306.

2. *Ibid.*, p. 300.

3. Alice Brown at times proclaimed herself a Unitarian; the characters in her novels constantly proclaim that they lack formal religious beliefs. According to the Reverend Lelen's letter to the Hon. and Mrs. Santen, she did ask to be formally received into the Catholic Church at the end of her life.

4. Agnes Repplier, "Fantasy," *The Commonweal*, XVI (May 18, 1932), 79.

5. *Bromley Neighborhood* (New York, 1917) p. 372.

6. Sweeney, p. 547.

7. Alice Brown, unpublished postcard to the Reverend Lelen, July 25, 1944.

Selected Bibliography

PRIMARY SOURCES

1. Novels.

The Day of His Youth. Boston and New York: Houghton, Mifflin and Company, 1897. A novelette.

Kings End. Boston and New York: Houghton, Mifflin and Company, 1901.

Margaret Warrener. Boston and New York: Houghton, Mifflin and Company, 1901.

Paradise. Boston and New York: Houghton, Mifflin and Company, 1905.

Rose MacLeod. Boston and New York: Houghton, Mifflin and Company, 1908.

The Story of Thyrza. Boston and New York: Houghton Mifflin and Company, 1909.

John Winterbourne's Family. Boston and New York: Houghton Mifflin and Company, 1910.

My Love and I. New York: The Macmillan Company, 1912.

The Prisoner. New York: The Macmillan Company, 1916.

Bromley Neighborhood. New York: The Macmillan Company, 1917.

The Black Drop. New York: The Macmillan Company, 1919.

The Wind Between the Worlds. New York: The Macmillan Company, 1920.

Old Crow. New York: The Macmillan Company, 1922.

Dear Old Templeton. New York: The Macmillan Company, 1927.

The Kingdom in the Sky. New York: The Macmillan Company, 1932.

Jeremy Hamlin. New York: D. Appleton-Century Company, 1934.

The Willoughbys. New York and London: D. Appleton-Century Company, Inc., 1935.

2. Volumes of Short Stories.

Meadow-Grass: Tales of New England Life. Boston and New York: Houghton, Mifflin and Company, 1895. Reprinted in 1969 by

the Garrett Press American Short Story Series. Selected for reprinting by Professor Clarence Gohdes for the Americans in
Fiction Series.

Tiverton Tales. Boston and New York: Houghton, Mifflin and Com-
pany, 1895. Reprinted in 1967 by the Gregg Press, Ridgewood,
New Jersey. Selected for reprinting by Professor Clarence
Gohdes for the Americans in Fiction Series.

High Noon. Boston and New York: Houghton, Mifflin and Company, 1904. Reprinted in 1970 in the Short Story Index Reprint
Series by Books for Libraries Press.

The County Road. Boston and New York: Houghton, Mifflin and
Company, 1906. Reprinted in 1968 by the Gregg Press, Ridge-
wood, New Jersey. Selected for reprinting by Professor
Clarence Gohdes for the Americans in Fiction Series.

Country Neighbors. Boston and New York: Houghton Mifflin
Company, 1910.

The One-Footed Fairy and Other Stories. Boston and New York:
Houghton Mifflin Company, 1911.

Vanishing Points. New York: The Macmillan Company, 1913. Reprinted in 1970 in the Short Story Index Reprint Series by
Books for Libraries Press.

The Flying Teuton. New York: The Macmillan Company, 1918.

Homespun and Gold. New York: The Macmillan Company, 1920.

3. Plays.

Children of Earth, A Play of New England. New York: The Macmillan Company, 1915.

One Act Plays. New York: The Macmillan Company, 1921.

Charles Lamb, A Play. New York: The Macmillan Company, 1924.

Pilgrim's Progress. Boston: privately printed, 1944.

4. Poetry.

The Road to Castaly. Boston: Copeland and Day, 1896.

The Road to Castaly (with Added Poems). New York: The Macmillan Company, 1917.

Ellen Prior. New York: The Macmillan Company, 1923.

5. Miscellaneous.

Three Heroines of New England Romance (with Louise Imogen
Guiney and Harriet Prescott Spofford). Boston: Little Brown
and Company, 1894.

Robert Louis Stevenson: A Study (with Louise Imogen Guiney).
   Boston: Copeland and Day (Issued for private distribution),
   1895.
By Oak and Thorn. Boston and New York: Houghton, Mifflin and
   Company, 1896.
Mercy Warren. New York: Charles Scribner's Sons, 1896. Issued
   in the Women of Colonial and Revolutionary Times Series.
   Spartanburg, South Carolina: Reprint Company, 1968.
Louise Imogen Guiney: A Study. New York: The Macmillan Com-
   pany, 1921.

SECONDARY SOURCES

*(Aside from Dr. Toth's doctoral dissertation, critical material
on Alice Brown is sparse.)*
ALICE BROWN. Pamphlet published by the Macmillan Company,
   probably in 1927, containing sketches of her life, short quota-
   tions from reviews of her books, and a thumbnail autobiograph-
   ical sketch.
COWIE, ALEXANDER. *The Rise of the American Novel.* New York:
   American Book Company, 1951. Explains local-color tech-
   nique and provides an excellent view of the development of the
   American novel.
OVERTON, GRANT. *The Women Who Make Our Novels.* New York:
   Moffat, Yard and Company, 1922, 49–54 (Reprinted in Essay
   Reprint Series Books for Freeport, New York: Libraries Press,
   Inc., 1967.) Brief critical analysis of some of her novels with
   some biographical material.
PATTEE, FRED LEWIS. *The New American Literature, 1890–1930.*
   New York and London: The Century Company, 1930, 316–18.
   Contains some critical analysis; shows how her magazine ex-
   perience affected her writing.
SCUDDER, HORACE. "Half a Dozen Story Books," *The Atlantic
   Monthly,* LXXVI (October, 1895), 554–59. Analyzes the dif-
   ference between the writing of Miss Brown and that of Mrs.
   Stowe, Miss Wilkins, Miss Jewett and others of this time.
SWEENEY, FRANCIS A. "Friend of Lou Guiney's," *America,* LXXX
   (1949), 546–47. Moving account of interview with Miss Brown
   shortly before her death; attests to the courage and hope which
   motivated her life.
THOMPSON, CHARLES MINER. "The Short Stories of Alice Brown,"
   The Atlantic Monthly, XCVIII (July, 1906), 55-65. Indicates the

main theme of Miss Brown's short stories, the women jilted in love; relates Miss Brown's obsession with romantic love to a lack in her artistry.

TOTH, SUSAN ERICKSON ALLEN. "More than Local-color: A Reappraisal of Rose Terry Cooke, Mary Wilkins Freeman and Alice Brown." Unpublished doctoral dissertation, University of Minnesota, 1969. Excellent study of the short stories of Alice Brown; emphasizes her mastery of this genre.

————. "Alice Brown (1857–1948)," *American Literary Realism 1870–1920*, V, 2 (Spring, 1972), 134–43. Excellent bibliographical article; covers history of Alice Brown criticisms, editions, reprints, and published manuscript material; also a review of areas needing critical attention.

WALKER, DOROTHEA Critical review of *Tiverton Tales* in *Library Newsletter*, Nassau Community College, V, 6 (March, 1970), 3–4. Relates the values in these tales to sought-for values today as well as showing the perspective of Miss Brown's art.

————. Critical review of *The County Road* in *Library Newsletter*, Nassau Community College, V, 8 (May, 1970), 4. Emphasizes Miss Brown's insight into human problems stemming from insensitivity in human relationships.

WILLIAMS, BLANCHE COLTON. *Our Short Story Writers* New York: Moffat, Yard, and Company, 1926. Reprinted in Essay Reprint Series Books. Freeport, New York: Libraries Press, Inc., 1969. Assesses Miss Brown from the standpoint of the authenticity of her tales; gives some evaluation of the volumes of short stories.

Index

Index

ABOUT THE AUTHOR

Dorothea Walker received a Bachelor's degree from Hunter College of the City University of New York and a Master's degree and a Ph.D. from St. John's University, Hillcrest.

John Phillips Marquand was the subject of Dr. Walker's dissertation and of a study which appeared in the *Nassau Review*. Besides her scholarly work, Dorothea Walker's activities have included serving as panelist for the Nassau-Queens English Association, college representative for the Nassau English Council, and participant in a recent AAUP Conference on Women in Academe. At present she is Professor of English at Nassau Community College, State University of New York.